Simon des Saints Joseph

The wonders of the heart of St. Teresa of Jesus

those first observed and also those of more recent date

Simon des Saints Joseph

The wonders of the heart of St. Teresa of Jesus
those first observed and also those of more recent date

ISBN/EAN: 9783741189821

Manufactured in Europe, USA, Canada, Australia, Japa

Cover: Foto ©Lupo / pixelio.de

Manufactured and distributed by brebook publishing software (www.brebook.com)

Simon des Saints Joseph

The wonders of the heart of St. Teresa of Jesus

Preface to the First American Edition.

This book was written originally in Italian, and first published under the direction of Mgr. Vaccari, Bishop Administrator of Nicotera and President of the Italian Committee for the Tercentenary of St. Teresa. It has been widely diffused in Europe, and, we think, should be well received in this country, as the subject of which it treats cannot fail to prove interesting to all who are disposed to admire and revere the wonderful works of God in His Saints.

At Alba de Tormes, Spain, in the monastery where St. Teresa died, her holy heart has been venerated during the past three centuries. It is preserved in a crystal urn, through which may be plainly seen the wound made by the Seraph when he transpierced the heart with a flaming dart.

Many wonderful things have been remarked at different periods in connection with this holy heart—such as the breaking of the glass of the Reliquary several times, without any apparent cause, so that it was found necessary to pierce several apertures in the upper part of the case; a notable increase in the size of the heart on various occasions; marvellous apparitions in the heart, etc. In the year 1836 two *thorns* were discovered growing out of the heart, and, up to the present date, at least fifteen have made their appearance. Other phenomena have also been observed. In the year 1875, M. Cardellach, a Spanish priest of the Congregation of the Mission, made a careful examination of the holy heart, and this book gives the result of his investigations.

TO THE
Children and Devoted Clients of Saint Teresa:

My dear ones, it is three hundred years since the heart of our holy Mother beat with the pulse of life, its palpitations have ceased until the consummation of ages, until the resurrection of the dead. Her blessed soul ascended to Heaven in the form of a dove, but her holy heart remains among us.

Though the great and generous soul once animating it be flown, it appears as if Divine Love which made here its favorite dwelling, had never been withdrawn. This little volcano (if we may use the expression), sending forth such flames during Teresa's life, was not extinguished by death. These flames slumbered a long time; but, as you will learn in the course of this work, more than once have they burst forth into life and activity.

To-day, this little volcano is surrounded by ashes and tiny stones, like our Vesuvius of Naples. From these ashes spring forth thorns, and with the thorns, much that will excite your admiration. To bring to light these later Wonders of Teresa's heart, binding them in one sheaf with those of an earlier date, is the aim and scope of my most humble work.

A dissemination of the knowledge of these marvels, now awaiting the Church's judgment, appears to me an excellent means of preparing all minds and hearts for the solemn celebration of the Third Centenary of our Saint's death.

My work is an answer, though a very imperfect one, to the appeal in the *Unita Cattolica*, of October 21, 1880, by Giovanni Bonetti, a priest of the Congregation of St. Francis de Sales, to Catholic writers and printers, urging them to prepare the people for the celebration of this most blessed Centenary.

I earnestly beg this excellent priest of St. Francis de Sales, likewise the editor of *L'Etoile du Carmel*, the editor of *Dévot à Saint Joseph*, the sons and daughters of St. Teresa,—all her clients of both sexes to aid me in the circulation of this little book.

Let each propose to himself the dissemination of a certain number of copies, and he will not fail of accomplishing it.

Let us put our hand to the work, and may the blessing of God be with us!

TO HIS EXCELLENCY THE MOST REVEREND

MGR. FREDERICO MASCARETTI,

*Of the Holy Order of Discalced Carmelites,
Former Bishop of Susa.*

MOST ILLUSTRIOUS MGR.

I am spending a few hours at Venice with the Discalced Carmelite Fathers, on the eve of the Feast of our great and holy Mother Teresa. The desire of pleasing a friend having a second time brought me to this wonderful city of Lagoons, the fact of being here has inspired me with the thought of giving to the world, under St. Mark's auspices, a modest work upon the heart of our holy Mother. And then I asked myself to whom it should be dedicated, or rather, who would be willing to accept the dedication of a book possessing no other merit than the subject of which it treats.

I at once thought of you, Most Reverend Mgr.—you have so many claims upon my esteem and affection, being the son of St. Teresa, one of the glories of her illustrious Order, and moreover, clothed with the Episcopal dignity. We are natives of the same country, we were educated at the same seminary, the same college, and you were, for a long time, a member of the Community of Carmel of Ferrara, which was always especially dear to me.

And it is thus, my book, which the Carmelite nuns of this city (Venice) have urged me to publish, will first see the light of day in the midst of its own family. May it, with God's benediction, prepare the minds and hearts of His people for the proper observance of the Saint's glorious Centenary, which, please God, we are going to celebrate in the month of October, 1882, two years hence.

Give me your blessing in God's name and that of our holy Mother, and believe me, very dear Mgr., your most humble servant and *confrere*,

   SIMON OF STS. JOSEPH AND TERESA,
    Priest of the 3rd Order of Discalced Carmelites.

VENICE, October 14, 1880.

EXPLANATION OF THE ENGRAVING.

FRONT.

2. Respiratory apertures pierced in the lid of the globe containing the heart.
4. Wire attached to the lid and sustaining the heart.
6. Wound of the Transverberation made by the Seraph.
8. Sanguineous ramification.
10. A collection of white grains resembling pearls or grains of sand.
12. Little wound made by the Seraph.
14. Membranous tissue covering the whole heart and very unevenly wrinkled.
16. A sort of thread with a knot, and another projection of the same nature very near it.
18. Great thorn with a point.
20. Shreds resembling wool or cloth.
22. Deposit of dust, residuum or sediment.
24. Interior view of bottom of crystal globe.

---

1. Lid in the form of a golden crown covering the top of the globe.
3. Crystal globe with dust scattered here and there upon the inner sides.
5. Heart of St. Teresa suspended by metallic wires.
7. A kind of brilliant of a blue color bordering upon purple.
9. Black spots resembling pieces of tobacco.
11. Membranes resembling ivy roots, over all the superficies of the heart.
13. Wrinkles in various places resembling stones in marquetry.
15. Little root growing immediately from the heart.
17. Shoot growing horizontally from the heart.
19. Great thorn with point.
21. Third thorn with double point.
23. Place whence the thorns start.
25. Group of five very fine thorns.

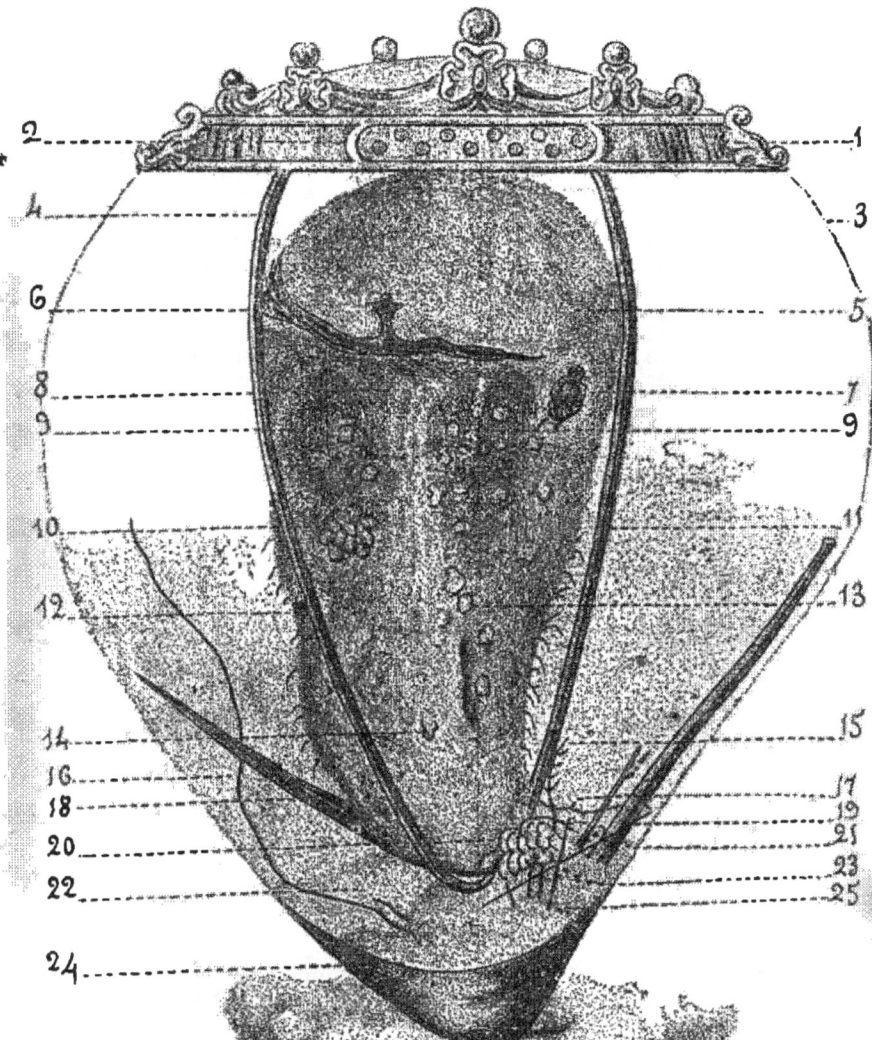

EXPLANATION OF THE ENGRAVING.

BACK.

2. Respiratory apertures pierced in the lid of the globe.
4. Wires attached to the lid and suspending the heart.
6. Heart of St. Teresa suspended by the wires.
8. Slight pricks probably made by the Seraph.
10. Wounds made by the Seraph.
12. Group of wrinkles resembling stones, or protuberances here and there, all over the surface of the heart.
14. Great thorn without point.
16. Third thorn with double point.
18. Little branch growing immediately from the heart.
20. Shoot growing horizontally from the heart.
22. Fourth thorn springing up very near the great thorn with one point.
24. Point whence the thorns seem to spring.
26. Little root growing between the crystal and the great pointed thorn.
28. Indentation or black segment.

---

1. Lid in the form of a golden crown covering the top of the globe.
3. Crystal globe with dust scattered upon the inside.
5. Extremity (right side) of the wound made by the Seraph.
7. Cavity apparently produced by an incision, or the extraction of a small portion of the heart.
9. Membranes like tiny roots of ivy, growing from all parts of the surface of the heart.
11. A sort of thread with knot, and another projection of a similar nature springing up very near it.
13. Wrinkled membrane enveloping nearly the whole heart.
15. Great thorn with point; from its root springs another thorn growing horizontally.
17. Shreds resembling clippings of cloth or wool.
19. Deposit of dust, residuum or sediment.
21. Two long slender thorns almost touching the bottom of the globe.
23. Two short thorns nearly parallel and perpendicular.
25. Short black thorn, which seen from the front appears like a point.
27. Bottom of the crystal vase or globe.

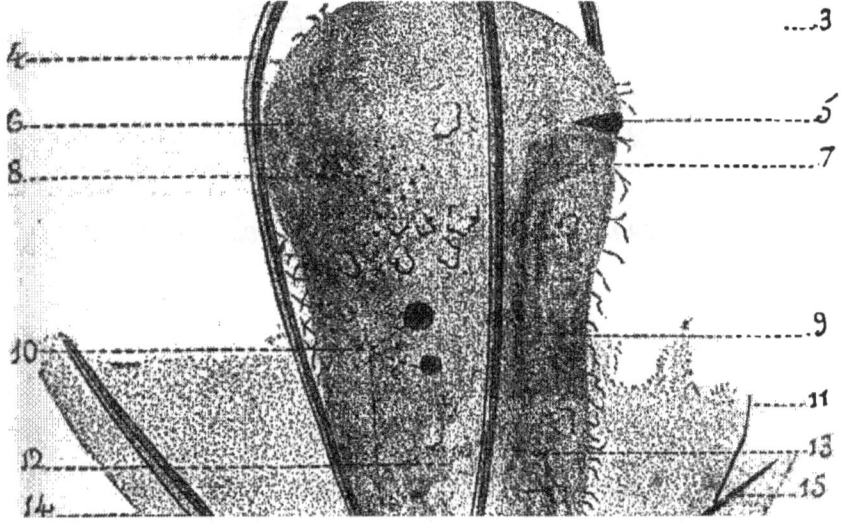

THE WONDERS
OF THE
HEART OF ST. TERESA OF JESUS.

THE EARLY WONDERS AND THOSE OF RECENT DATE.

FIRST PART.
THE EARLY WONDERS.

I.

The Heart of Jesus as Shown to the Blessed Margaret Mary. The Heart of St. Teresa Resembling that of Jesus.

Mgr. Jean Joseph Languet, Bishop of Soissons, in his "Life of the Blessed Margaret Mary Alacoque," beatified in 1864 by Pius IX, recounts as follows one of the most astonishing revelations with which the illustrious servant of God was favored: "God," says he, "never leaves unrewarded the sacrifices we make for Him, and He wished to crown the fidelity of His servant by new favors. I shall mention one of the most remarkable, and as it is especially connected with devotion to the Heart of Jesus, I shall use the very words of the servant of God when relating it to her director:

"'After receiving my Divine Saviour on the Feast of St. John the Evangelist, He deigned to accord me a grace, somewhat, it appears to me, of the same nature as that bestowed upon His beloved disciple. I beheld the Heart of Jesus upon a throne of flames, from all sides of which emanated rays more resplendent than the sun and as transparent as crystal. The wound He received upon the cross was distinctly visible, likewise a crown of thorns around this Divine Heart, and above it a cross, which seemed to be fixed therein. My Divine Master made me understand that these instruments of His Passion were emblematic of His exceeding love for man, which had been the cause of all His sufferings,—that from the first moment of His Incarnation these sufferings had been ever before Him, and the cross as it were imbedded in His Heart,—that from this first moment even, He accepted the agonies and humiliations His most holy Humanity would undergo during His mortal life; also, the outrages to which this same love for the human race would expose Him to the very end of ages, since He ever remains with us in the Blessed Sacrament.'"[1]

---

[1] Book VII, number 93.

This revelation of the blessed daughter of St. Francis de Sales has become the immutable type of infinite representations of the Sacred Heart of Jesus, exposed in our churches to the veneration of the faithful. Cannot our pious readers find in the heart of the Seraphic Mother, St. Teresa, a *very unusual* resemblance to that of her Divine Spouse? We say *very unusual*, but no such striking resemblance has *ever* been discovered in the heart of any other saint. At Alba de Tormes, in Spain, this incomparable virgin's heart has been, for three centuries, an object of more than admiration. It is enclosed in a crystal case, and exposed upon a sort of throne; it has a wound, also its thorns and a cross. These divers objects are disposed in a manner different from those in the Heart of Jesus, yet they form sufficient resemblance, together with the marvels of which we are about to speak, to frame for our Saint a panegyric, the most extraordinary, the most astonishing—a panegyric, written in a measure, by the hand of God Himself. We have said all when we say that the heart of Teresa resembles that of Jesus as much as the heart of a poor creature, purified and exalted by grace, can resemble the Heart of its God. "It is useless," said St. Ambrose, "seeking praises afar, for an object under one's eyes bearing its own praises." *Prolixa laudatio est, quæ non quæritur sed tenetur.*[1]

God has likewise wrought great wonders in the hearts of a few other saints, for example, in Gertrude's, Magdalen of Pazzi's, Francis Carracciolo's, and especially in those of the two chosen virgins, the blessed Clare of Montefalco, an Augustinian, and St. Veronica Juliana, a Capuchin. The hearts of these last two being opened after death, miraculously engraven upon them were found the principal instruments of our Lord's Passion. This certainly was for them a great and especial glory; and yet though not desirous of drawing useless comparisons, we must say that the resemblance between Jesus's Heart and that of the *ecstatic* Castilian is unparalleled and astonising.

II.

Chronological Table of the Life and Foundations of St. Teresa.

Before occupying ourselves with the Wonders (as to whether they are natural or supernatural) God has wrought in our holy Mother Teresa's heart, we must make our readers acquainted with the principal events of her long life, but wishing

---

[1] De virg. lib. 1.

our book to be as brief as possible, we shall give merely a chronological abridgment of them.

Teresa was born on Wednesday, March 28, 1515, at half-past five in the morning, and was baptized the same day in the Parish Church of St. John of Avila, a city of Old Castile.

1522—Thirsting for martyrdom, she leaves the paternal roof in company with her brother Rodrigo, to go among the Moors.

1529—Her fervor in God's service grows cool.

1531—She enters as a scholar the Augustinian monastery of Avila, where she soon recovers her lost fervor.

1532—She falls sick and returns to her family.

1533—On the 2d of November, Feast of All Souls, she renounces the world and enters the Carmelite Convent of the Incarnation at Avila.

1534—On the 3d of November she makes her solemn profession.

1535—She falls sick again, and is taken by her excellent father into the country, where she gives herself up to mental prayer.

1536—She returns to her father's house, and thence to the Convent of the Incarnation.

1539—She is miraculously cured by St. Joseph. She neglects mental prayer.

1542—She resumes the practice of it and perseveres therein, notwithstanding the most painful aridity.

1556—God bestows upon her supernatural gifts.

1557—She is directed by the Fathers of the Society of Jesus. She has a conference with St. Francis Borgia.

1558—She has frequent heavenly communicacations. Gift of visions, *intellectual* and *imaginary*.

In this first period of St. Teresa's life, embracing about forty-three years, we perceive in her heart a continual struggle of divine grace, which is sometimes victorious, sometimes repelled, yet never vanquished, our Lord Himself assuring her of this latter fact, as she recounts in her writings, which Father Bouix has carefully studied in the original.

The following years of her life embrace those of her wonderful Foundations:

1559—Her visions become more frequent. First idea of founding a monastery. She is visited by St. Peter of Alcantara. Memorable year of the *Transverberation* of her heart, the subject of this work.

1560—She makes a vow of doing in all things that which seems to her most perfect. Sore interior trials. She is occupied with the foundation of the new monastery.

1561—She restores to life one of her nephews.

1562—She finishes at Toledo the first account of her life. The 24th of August, she founds at

Avila the first monastery of the Reformed Carmelites and consecrates it to St. Joseph.

1563-1566—She writes in this new monastery the second account of her life and "The Way of Perfection."

1567—The General of the Carmelites visits her and authorizes her to found new houses. She immediately founds that of Medina del Campo. First interview of the Saint with St. John of the Cross at Medina. She goes to Alcala.

1568—New monasteries at Malagon and Valladolid; first convent of the Discalced Carmelite Friars at Durvelo.

1569—Foundation of religious houses for women at Toledo and Pastrana; also a monastery for men at Pastrana. The Saint spends nearly all this year at Toledo, absenting herself only to make a few short journeys.

1570—The convent of Durvelo is closed and the inmates sent to Manzera. The Saint quits Toledo and goes to Salamanca to found a monastery there. Foundation of a monastery at Alcala for men.

1571—Foundation of the house at Alba for nuns. The Saint is made Prioress of the Convent of the Incarnation at Avila, and assumes her charge in the month of October amidst the gravest difficulties. Foundation of a monastery for men at Altomira.

1572—Foundation of the friary, called Our Lady of Succor.

1573—Another foundation of the same kind at Granada and Pegnuela. The Saint is sent to Salamanca where she begins to write her book of the "Foundations."

1574—The Carmelites (men) at Seville. The nuns of Pastrana leave their monastery and repair to Segovia about the beginning of April.

1575—Foundation of convents for women at Veas and Seville, one for men at Almodovar.

1576—Foundation of religious (women) at Caravacca. The Saint withdraws to Toledo where, until the 14th of November, she continues her work upon "The History of the Foundations." The Chapter of Discalced Carmelites orders the translation of the Convent of Pegnuela to Calvary, near Veas.

1577—June 2, the Saint commences writing her book, "The Interior Castle;" in July, she leaves Toledo for Avila, and arriving there places the monastery of St. Joseph under the jurisdiction of the Order. She finishes "The Interior Castle" November 29.

1578—Persecutions against the Reform of Carmel gravely threatening its existence.

1579—April 1, the Discalced Carmelites are detached from the jurisdiction of the Mitigated Carmelites. The government of the former is confided to Father Angelo de Salazar, a Mitigated Carmelite, but very favorable towards the Reform. In the month of June, the Saint is sent from Toledo to several other monasteries. Saint John of the Cross founds a convent at Baeza.

1580—Foundation of a monastery for women at Villanueva de la Jara. New journeys of our holy Mother. Brief of Gregory XIII, dated June 22, erecting the Discalced Carmelites of both sexes into a separate province, with its own Provincial, immediately subject to the General of the whole Order. Foundation at Palencia.

1581—Foundation of the monastery for men at Valladolid, of the college of Salamanca, and of a convent for women at Soria. Father Gratian of the Mother of God elected first Provincial of the Reform. The holy Mother elected Prioress of St. Joseph's of Avila.

1582—Foundation of a house for nuns at Granada, by the venerable Mother Anne of Jesus; of a monastery at Lisbon for men, and at Burgos for women. The holy Mother Teresa returning from this last foundation, falls sick, the 20th of September, in the monastery of Alba de Tormes, where she dies about nine o'clock in the evening of October 5, after an ecstacy of fourteen hours. The introduction of the Gregorian calendar beginning this day, consequently, the next, consecrated to her funeral ceremonies (celebrated with great solemnity) was called the 15th of the month.

The Saint was sixty-seven years, six months and seven days old. She had worn the religious habit forty-six years, twenty-six of which she had spent at the convent of the Incarnation at Avila. The last twenty years of her life had been consecrated to the reform of the Order, established in thirty-two houses, seventeen of women and fifteen of men, and constituting a Province.

III.

A Chronological Table of Facts Connected with the Body of St. Teresa.

1583—July 4, her sepulchre was opened for the first time—the body was found incorrupt, perfect and exhaling a delightful perfume.

1585—November 24, by order of the Superiors of the province, the Saint's body is taken in the night from its tomb in the monastery of Alba, and carried to that of Avila.

1586—January 1, her body is visited by the Bishop of Avila. Sixtus V, at the solicitation of the Dukes of Alba, orders the precious relic to be taken back to Alba, which was complied with on the 23d of August.

1589—After an attentive consideration of the various arguments of the respective cities and monasteries of Alba and Avila, each urging its claim to the Saint's body, Sixtus V, on the 10th of July, decreed its remaining at Alba.

1591—The Bishop of Salamanca visits this sacred relic.

1595—Commencement of the investigation of the holy Mother's Life and Miracles.

1598—The Saint's body is put in a chapel in a more conspicuous place, so as to be within the reach of the veneration of the faithful.

1614—April 24, Mother Teresa of Jesus is Beatified.

1616—The holy Mother's sarcophagus is enclosed in a marble urn and removed to a new chapel dedicated to her.

1622—March 12, solemn Canonization of the holy Mother by Gregory XV.

1629—The holy Mother's paternal home is transformed into a church and a friary for Discalced Carmelites.

1750—Another and last inspection of the Saint's body; it is still flexible and exhaling celestial perfumes.

1760—The sacred deposit is enclosed in a new reliquary of silver and placed upon the magnificent altar where the faithful venerate it at the present day.

To complete this chronological picture, we will add, that during the civil wars agitating Spain in 1835, the year witnessing the formation of the thorns under the Saint's heart, the Carmelites feared some profanation of their holy treasure, and several illustrious personages urged upon the Spanish government the necessity of taking proper measures for its prevention. The Saint's body still reposes in the monastery of her Order at Alba, in the Diocese of Salamanca, but the precious gifts and offerings made the Saint by Catholics sovereigns and the grandees of Spain, among them the Duchess of Alba, have disappeared, sacrilegious hands, as is ever the case in revolutions, having seized upon them. The body itself was respected, and an unwilling witness of this sacrilegious spoliation affirms, that it was then, two centuries and a half after death, in a state of perfect preservation and as flexible as in life. It is enclosed in a double urn of crystal, surrounded by a silver grating locked by three keys, one of which is in possession of the religious at the monastery, another is kept by the Duke of Alba, and a third by the king. At least it was thus in the month of March, 1840.

Near the little river Adaja, contiguous to Avila, a small chapel has been erected on the spot where Teresa and her brother Rodrigo were arrested by their uncle, as they were escaping to the country of the Moors, in hopes of there winning the palm of martyrdom.

After these short preliminaries, we now arrive at the especial subject of this book.

IV.

God Prepares Teresa's Heart for the Marvel of the Transverberation.

If the nature of the mind and the manner in which its thoughts are engendered have ever been for man an impenetrable mystery, is not his heart equally mysterious? We read in Job " that God hath made an infinity of great and unsearchable and wonderful things:" *Qui facit magna et inscrutabilia et mirabilia absque numero.*[1] And we are forced to admit, with Jeremias and the author of Proverbs, that the human heart is one of those creations enveloped in the deepest obscurity: *Pravum est cor omnium et inscrutabile: quis cognoscet illud?*[2] God has chosen it as the principal field of the operations of His grace. Admitting, then, its impenetrability, there is nothing astonishing in the fact that very many

---

[1] Job v., 9; xxxvii, 5.
[2] Jeremias xvii., 9; Proverbs xxv., 3.

of these works of grace remain a mystery. And
God, wishing to give man a sensible proof of
His action upon the hearts of some Saints, has
made these hearts after death the scene of marvels
apparent to the senses; and thus the visible proof
of invisible marvels: *argumentum non apparentium*, says St. Paul.[1]

We have said that Christ chooses man's heart
as the principal field of the operations of His
grace, making it fertile and luxuriant to Eternal
life. Faith, hope and charity are indeed three
plants which here germinate, blossom and bear
fruit, as we learn from the Holy Scriptures.
Says St. Paul, speaking of faith: "With the
heart we believe unto justice, but with the mouth
confession is made unto salvation:" *Corde creditur ad justitiam: ore autem confessio fit ad salutem;*[2] and David, of the hope of the just,
considering it an act of the heart, which is the
seat of hope: *Paratum cor ejus sperare in domino.*[3] Again, St. Paul, speaking of charity, says
"that it proceeds from a pure heart:" *Finis autem præcepti est caritas de corde puro.*[4] The
same could be said of all the other virtues—of
humility, simplicity, obedience.

---

[1] The evidence of things that appear not.—*Heb. xi.*, 1.
[2] Rom. x., 10.
[3] Ps. cxi., v., 7.
[4] I Timothy, i., 5.

There is no doubt, then, that if God's grace wrought wonders in St. Teresa, her heart was the scene of these wonders, and hence we must not be astonished if it still appears in the eyes of all who contemplate it as a perpetual miracle. But the greatest marvel of her heart, was that fire of charity which consumed it for sixty-seven years, causing her the most varying emotions; and we believe that the phenomena of this organ after death, were intended as a perpetual testimony to the flame of ardent love existing therein, even ere the angel had pierced it with his fiery dart.

Let us listen to her own description of her spiritual life previous to this prodigy of grace. We quote the following from the XXIX Chapter of her autobiography, written at the command of her confessors:

"When they had begun to insist on my putting my visions to a test like this, and resisting them, the graces I received were multiplied more and more. I tried to distract myself; I never ceased to be in prayer. Even during sleep my prayer seemed to be continual. . . . . Not long afterwards His Majesty began, according to His promise, to make it clear that it was He Himself who appeared, by the growth in me of the love of God so strong, that I know not who could have infused it; for it was most supernatural,

and I had not attained to it by any efforts of my
own. I saw myself dying of a desire to see God,
and I knew not how to seek that life otherwise
than by dying. Certain impetuosities of love,
though not so intolerable as those of which I
have spoken before, nor yet of so great worth,
overwhelmed me. I knew not what to do; for
nothing gave me pleasure, and I had no control
over myself. It seemed as if my soul were really
torn away from myself. O supreme artifice of
our Lord! how tenderly didst Thou deal with
Thy miserable slave! Thou didst hide Thyself
from me, and didst yet constrain me with Thy
love—with a death so sweet that my soul would
never wish it over. ... It is not possible for
any one to understand those impetuosities if he
has not experienced them himself. They are not
an upheaving of the breast, nor those devotional
sensations, not uncommon, which seem on the
point of causing suffocation, and are beyond
control. ... These other impetuosities are very
different. It is not we who apply the fuel. The
fire is already kindled, and we are thrown into
it in a moment to be consumed. It is by no
efforts of the soul that it sorrows over the wound
which the absence of our Lord has inflicted on
it. It is far otherwise; *for an arrow is driven
into the entrails to the very quick, and into the
heart at times,* so that the soul knows not what

is the matter with it, nor what it wishes for. It understands clearly enough that it wishes for God, and that the arrow seems tempered with some herb which makes the soul hate itself for the love of our Lord, and willingly lose its life for Him. It is impossible to describe or explain *the way in which God wounds the soul,* nor the very grievous pain inflicted, which deprives it of all self-consciousness; yet this pain is so sweet that there is no joy in the world which gives greater delight. As I have just said, the soul would wish to be always dying of this wound. This pain and this bliss together carried me out of myself, and I never could understand how it was. . . . Oh! how often do I remember when in this state, those words of David: 'As the hart panteth after the fountains of water, so my soul panteth after Thee, O God.' They seem to me to be literally true of myself. . . . When these impetuosities are not very violent, they seem to admit of a little mitigation—at least the soul seeks some relief, because it knows not what to do—through certain penances, the painfulness of which, and even the shedding of its blood, are no more felt than if the body were dead. The soul seeks for ways and means to do something that may be felt, for the love of God; but the first pain is so great, that no bodily torture I know of can take it away. As relief is not to be had here, these medicines are too mean for so high a disease. Some slight mitigation may be had, and the pain may pass away a little, by praying God to relieve its sufferings; but the soul sees no relief except in death, by which it thinks to attain completely to the fruition of its good. At other times, these impetuosities are so violent, that the soul can neither do this nor anything else; the whole body is contracted, and neither hand nor foot can be moved. If the body be upright at the time, it falls down, as a thing that has no control over itself."[1]

Such is the faithful picture St. Teresa has traced of her spiritual condition. It was thus our Lord prepared her for the prodigy of the Transverberation.

V.

Doctrine of the Holy Scriptures and the Doctors of the Church Upon the Interior Wound of the Heart.

We earnestly desire our pious readers to be fully enlightened upon the subject before us, and for this purpose, 'ere touching upon the marvel

---

[1] The above is a *verbatim* extract from a very accurate and highly-approved translation of her life from the original Spanish by Lewis, published in London.

itself, we direct their attention to some reflections which may be useful. The Holy Scriptures, both of the Old and New Testament, represent the Incarnate Son of God under the figure of an archer. "Thy arrows are pointed," says the Prophet David: *sagittæ tuæ acutæ, populi sub te cadent, in corda inimicorum regis.* "Thy penetrating arrows," translates Mgr. Martini, "shall pierce the heart of the enemies of the king, and the people shall fall at thy feet." This Psalm no doubt refers to Our Lord Jesus Christ and His celestial nuptials with the Church. In the VI Chapter of the Apocalypse the Divine Archer predicted by David is contemplated in a vision. Says St. John: "And I saw: and behold a white horse, and he that sat on him had a bow, and there was a crown given him, and he went forth conquering that he might conquer." This horseman reappears in Chapter XIX, and is there clearly designated as the Word of God, the King of Kings, the Lord of Lords. Again, in the XLIX Chapter of Isaias, the future Messias is announced under the figure of a chosen arrow concealed in God's quiver. *Posuit me sicut sagittam electam in pharetra sua abscondit me.*

In the book of Sacred Canticles, on the contrary, the Divine Lover is represented as wounded in the heart by an arrow from the hand of the Spouse. *Vulnerasti cor meum, soror mea sponsa.*

But these arrows of the Spouse are her eyes and her hair. *Vulnerasti cor meum in uno oculorum tuorum, in uno crine colli tui.*[1]

These figurative expressions explain what has been written by Teresa of Jesus, who with heart deeply wounded by the piercing shafts of charity, had also the happiness of seeing her dear Jesus wounded with love for her.

The Fathers and Doctors of the Church, in their writings, have made various allusions to the wound of Divine Love in the soul. Origen says, in his homily on the Canticle of Canticles: "To be wounded by charity is beautiful and honorable. Some have felt the arrows of carnal love, some of terrestrial concupiscence. But as for thee, expose thy members and thy whole body to this dart, for it is God who lances it. Listen to the Scriptures speaking of this arrow, or rather that thy admiration may be boundless, hear what the arrow says of itself: 'He has taken me as a chosen arrow, He has guarded me in His quiver, and has said to me: "It is a great thing for thee to merit being called My servant."'"

In several passages of his works, especially in his Commentaries upon the Psalms, St. Augustine likewise speaks of this interior wound made in the soul by charity. We shall content ourselves

---

[1] Canticle of Canticles, iv.

with quoting a few words from his " Confessions." St. Teresa read them, and found them the source of much spiritual profit: " Thou hast wounded my heart with the arrows of Thy love, and I bore in my bowels Thy words which had pierced them."[1]

St. Francis de Sales, a Doctor of the Church, and a master on this point, speaks at considerable length of the spiritual wound of love, in the last three chapters of Book VI on the Love of God. The first chapter treats of *the wound of love*, the second of *another means by which Divine Love wounds hearts*, and the third of *the longings of a heart wounded by love*. Happy, a thousand times happy is he who not only reads and meditates upon these things for his edification, but likewise experiences them himself, for all becomes advantageous and useful to him who loves God, whilst naught avails him who loves not. "Add charity," says St. Augustine, " and all things are profitable." *Adde charitatem, prosunt omnia.*[2]

One motive inducing us to undertake this little work was the hope of inflaming our readers' hearts with this virtue of charity, of which the fathers and doctors of the Church have written such admirable things. We are grieved to per-

---

[1] Lib. ix Conf., ch. ii.
[2] Serm. 50 *de Verbis Domim.*

ceive amongst us the decline of the spiritual life, for with charity faint and languid it is impossible to please God.

VI.

The Prodigy of the Transverberation of Saint Teresa's Heart.

Transverberation is the name we call the wound in St. Teresa's heart, both because the Church in her liturgy uses this word, and also because we find it the most suitable expression. The following account is that given by the Holy Reformatrix herself:

"I saw an angel close by me, on my left side, in bodily form. This I am not accustomed to see, unless very rarely. Though I have visions of angels frequently, yet I see them only by an intellectual vision, such as I have spoken of before. It was our Lord's will that in this vision I should see the angel in this wise. He was not large, but small of stature, and most beautiful, his face burning, as if he were one of the highest angels, who seem to be all of fire: they must be those whom we call cherubims.[1] Their names

---

[1] In the MS. of the Saint, preserved in the Escurial, the word is "cherubines;" but all the editors before Don Vicente de la Fuente have adopted the suggestion in the mar-

they never tell me, but I see very well that there is in Heaven so great a difference between one angel and another, and between these and the others, that I cannot explain it. I saw in his hand a long spear of gold, and at the iron's point there seemed to be a little fire. He appeared to me to be thrusting it at times into my heart, and to pierce my very entrails; when he drew it out he seemed to draw them out also, and to leave me all on fire with a great love of God. The pain was so great that it made me moan; and yet so surpassing was the sweetness of this excessive pain that I could not wish to be rid of it. The soul is satisfied now with nothing less than God. The pain is not bodily, but spiritual, though the body has its share in it, even a large one. It is a caressing of love so sweet which now takes place between the soul and God, that I pray God of His goodness to make him experience it who may think that I am lying. During the days that this lasted, I went about as if beside myself. I wished to see, or speak, with no one, but only to cherish my pain, which was to me a greater bliss than all created things could give."

---

gin of Bānes, who preferred "seraphim." F. Bouix, in his translation, corrected the mistake, but, with his usual modesty, did not call the readers' attention to it.—*Note to the translation by David Lewis, from which this extract is taken.*

St. Teresa has elsewhere and in other terms described this wondrous wound. In one of her canticles, found in 1700 at the monastery of St. Joseph, of Seville, and which we shall translate as closely as possible from the Spanish, she thus expresses herself:

"I felt a sudden blow in the very depths of my entrails: it came from a Divine hand, for it operated great things in me. This blow wounded me, and although the wound be mortal and cause pain, the like of which there is not, it is a death bringing forth life. If it kills, how then does it give life? And if it gives life, how does it cause death? How does it heal in wounding? And how is it that one is united to the Author of the wound? Truly, so divine is His skill that in spite of the cruel peril, He issues triumphant from the proof, and operating great things."

It appears that Father Peretto had some knowledge of this canticle. After mentioning the wound the Holy Mother received from an angel, as she was contemplating the glory the saints acquired in Heaven by charity, he adds, that she often hummed a canticle. The words of this canticle resemble that found at Seville.

The better to explain St. Teresa's words when she says that she saw the angel who inflicted the wound, though ordinarily these celestial spirits did not appear to her in a manner perceptible to the senses, we will remark that the visions with which God favors his elect are divided into three classes: There are *intellectual, imaginary,* and *real* visions, these last being very rare. *Intellectual* visions address themselves entirely to the mind, without any image properly so called; *imaginary* visions are painted more or less vividly upon the imagination and are subject to numberless illusions; *real* visions strike the exterior senses, for instance, Abraham, Gideon and Manuel saw with their eyes of flesh God's angels. St. Teresa never had any of these corporeal visions, as she herself declares in her book, "Mansions of the Soul; or, the Interior Castle," and the vision of the angel that wounded her must, in consequence, have belonged to the second class.

The testimony of the holy Scriptures and numberless incidents of ecclesiastical history, all confirm the belief that God used the ministry of an angel in wounding St. Teresa's heart. To convince ourselves that such a prodigy was in no wise at variance with the Divine economy, we need but read the Apocalypse of St. John, plainly proving the intervention of angels in all the phenomena recounted by the Evangelist, whether of the natural or supernatural order.

We cannot finish this chapter ere drawing a parallel between the prodigies one Seraph wrought in St. Teresa's heart, and another in the body of St. Francis of Assisium. The poor man of Assisium recalls the poor religious of Avila much more strongly than one might at first suppose. They are as two musical instruments tuned in unison, or two pages of the same book. A Seraph, on Mount Alvernia, imprinted upon St. Francis' body the sacred Stigmata and Five Wounds of Jesus Christ. A Seraph in the cloister of the Incarnátion at Avila, imprinted in St. Teresa's heart, the Wound of the side of Jesus Christ. And thus the first reproduced in St. Francis all the marks of the exterior sufferings of the Son of God, and the second, in St. Teresa, all those of His interior sufferings. The one burned with love, and it burst forth in canticles, simple, it is true, but immortal. Likewise, the second, consumed with the ardors of a seraphic charity, gave vent to them in inspired verses, which are far dearer to the Spaniards than the twenty volumes of poems collected by Ramon Fernandez. Among all the Saints of the Western Church, it would be very difficult to find a man surpassing St. Francis of Assisium in sanctity, or a woman vanquishing Teresa in love.

VII.

Proofs of the Transverberation of St. Teresa's Heart.

The prodigy of which we speak is not one of those that a Catholic writer must approach most timidly, and with that extreme reserve inspired by fear of venturing upon dangerous ground. The judgment of the Church on the subject, and the actual state of the heart three centuries after death, render the fact certain and irrefutable. This heart has never known the corruption of the tomb; it is enshrined with profound veneration in the monastery of Reformed Carmelites at Alba de Tormes, in the Diocese of Salamanca, in the province of Leon, in the western part of Spain. Every year it is exposed to public veneration, and this exposition is the occasion of extraordinary solemnities, the devotion of the multitude manifesting itself by the rich decorations of the streets through which the heart, with the Saint's left arm, is carried in procession. An account of these details is given in her life written by Father Frederick of St. Anthony, a Discalced Carmelite.

In the last century, Father Joseph of the Holy Spirit, the author of a treatise on Mystical Theology, carefully examined the relic, and he declares that not only has it been wounded, but really transpierced, and the lips of the wound slightly burned. " I am astonished," he writes, " when I venerate in this *most sacred* heart, the lips of the wound not only open, but also partially burned. Do not think that the arrow merely wounded it, but know for certain that it passed through, for on both sides do we behold the aperture with its lips partly burned."[1]

Joseph Lopez Ezquerra, a learned and pious writer of Biscay in Spain, speaks thus in his "Mystical Lamp": "A Seraph with a flaming dart repeatedly pierced Teresa's heart; this vision as well as the wounds was true and real, as can be verified in a manner perceptible to the senses by her heart enshrined at Alba. The wound presents lips slightly burned by the Seraph's dart. The preservation of the natural life under these circumstances is no less miraculous than this interior wound itself, the chest remaining whole and intact."

But these testimonies and others of a similar nature are of slight weight compared to that rendered by the Roman Church, which, after a most severe examination, has not hesitated to

---

[1] The author of this pamphlet justly remarks, that we cannot approve of the epithet *most holy* as applied to St. Teresa's heart, such an expression being reserved solely for the adorable Heart of our Lord Jesus Christ.

solemnly declare its belief in the fact, expressing it both in the Office of the Breviary for October 15 and the Bull of Canonization published by Gregory XV. In the Fifth Lesson of Matins we read these words: "Her heart was consumed with such love of God that she merited to see an angel pierce it with a burning dart." *Tanto autem divini amoris incendio cor ejus conflagravit, ut merito viderit angelum ignito jaculo sibi præcordia transverberantem.*

And, in the Vesper Hymn, the Church hesitates not to congratulate this seraphic virgin, the Reformatrix of Carmel, upon so admirable a grace, which was to her ample compensation for having been denied the privilege of giving her life for Jesus in pagan lands. "It remains for thee to suffer a sweeter death," sings the Church. "Thou art called to more delightful sufferings. Thou shalt fall, wounded by an arrow of Divine Love."

> Sed te manet suavior
> Mors, pœna poscit dulcior:
> Divini amoris cuspide
> In vulnus icta concides.

We might say that this entire hymn, so beautiful in its simplicity, has no other object than to extol the Transverberation of the Holy Mother's Heart.

The Bull of Canonization is merely the official

and authentic abridgment of the rigorous examination preceding it. We quote a portion of its words in number XII:

"But among all Teresa's virtues her love of God shone most resplendent. It was such that her confessors celebrated and admired it not as the charity of a human being, but rather of a cherub. Our Lord Jesus Christ augmented this love in a wonderful manner by the numberless visions and revelations He showered upon her. On a certain occasion, extending to her His right hand and showing her one of the nails of His Passion, He chose her for His Spouse, and addressed her in these words: 'Henceforth, like a true spouse, thou shalt have charge of My honor. From this moment I am all thine and thou art all Mine!'"

"Another time she sees an angel pierce her heart with a burning dart. Then, so transported by these gifts and inspired by God, she makes the vow—very difficult, indeed, to accomplish—of doing always that which appears to her most perfect and most conducive to the greater glory of God."

After such irrefutable testimony, confirmed by the actual state of her heart at present, to doubt the miracle of the Transverberation, would be to deny at midday the existence of the sun. May it be permitted the lowliest of St. Teresa's sons to unite his voice with that of the Universal Church, congratulating her upon so grand a privilege, which places her among the most celebrated Saints and illustrious Virgins honored at our altars.

VIII.

Institution of an Especial Feast to Perpetuate the Memory of this Prodigy.

If ancient Carmel can justly claim the merit of having spread throughout the world devotion to the Blessed Virgin, and carried to the West devotion to the Patriarch St. Joseph, Reformed Carmel can add to these two glories a third, peculiarly its own—that of having excited in the hearts of the faithful, veneration and love for St. Teresa. We must not be astonished that, as the Church instituted an especial feast to honor the Sacred Stigmata of St. Francis of Assisium, the religious of Carmel have most earnestly endeavored to obtain the like favor, in perpetual remembrance of the Transverberation of their Seraphic Mother's Heart.

The immortal work of Benedict XIV on the Beatification and Canonization of the Servants of God may be profitably consulted on this subject. When the cause was agitated during the last century, he was then Archbishop of Theodosia, and fulfilled the difficult office of Promoter of the Faith.

In Book IV, chapter viii., No. 6 of his works, he thus expresses himself upon this question: "Among all the gifts by which God has been pleased to manifest Teresa's sanctity, the most wonderful is that of Divine Love, which so inflamed her soul, that she saw an angel pierce her heart with a burning dart, as we read in the Bull of Canonization by Gregory XIV, and in the Second Lessons of the Office, recited by the Universal Church October 15.

"When I was Promoter of the Faith," he continues, "the Discalced Carmelite Fathers of both families, that is, of both Spain and Italy, petitioned the Sacred Congregation to grant them the faculty of reciting, on the 27th day of August annually, as a double of the second class, with appropriate lessons, the office of the Transverberation of St. Teresa's Heart. Whilst fully admitting the reality of the celestial favor, I replied, that as the Fathers rested their petition upon the actual state of the heart enshrined in the monastery of the most holy Incarnation of Alba, affirming that the wound was still visible, it would be necessary to verify their assertion and have the heart submit to an examination, proving the evidence of the scar this wound has left.

I also mentioned instances in which, though great and indisputable favors had been accorded other saints, these favors were not commemorated by an office. The postulators having collected the legal proofs established the fact of the visible impression of the wound in the Saint's heart; they also enumerated instances showing that in certain churches a special office had been accorded the remembrance of favors bestowed on some saints, although these favors had been already commemorated in the office of the Saint's feast. Then on the 25th of May, 1726, with the approbation of the Sovereign Pontiff, Benedict XIII, the two families of Discalced Carmelites were granted an especial office, with its own lessons, on the feast of the Transverberation of St. Teresa's Heart."

We will add, that on the 17th of March, 1728, Pope Benedict XIII permitted allusion to be made to this Prodigy in the Breviary and Missal. Under Clement XII, by a decree of the Congregation of Rites, dated September 15, 1731, a favor similar to that of the two Carmelite families was accorded the imperial city of Vienna, and finally, on the 5th of December, 1733, this favor was extended to all Spain. We know not whether it will be granted the universal Church, according to the desire of her sons. They have already obtained from Benedict XIV, by rescript of August 8, 1744, a Plenary Indulgence for all who, on the 27th of August, visit a church of the Discalced Carmelites from the time of first Vespers.

IX.

Condition of St. Teresa's Heart in the last Century.

We earnestly desire to give in this little work all possible information concerning the seraphic Mother's heart, and for this purpose we shall begin by describing the state in which it was found when Benedict XIV, as we have just mentioned, submitted it to a judicial examination.

On the 25th of January, 1726, one hundred and fifty-five years ago, the Rev. Francis Anthony Spinosa, Vicar-General of Salamanca, visited officially at Alba the Saint's heart. He was accompanied by two physicians, a surgeon, and several important personages of Alba. After most careful and conscientious observation, with one accord, they all recognized the prodigy of the preservation of the heart as well as the wound still visible, and made their deposition under oath. From these numberless depositions we shall select that of the surgeon Emmanuel Sanchez He affirms that he saw in this heart, "a transversal rent or opening at the upper and anterior part, very narrow in width, and the superficies very slight; it has been proven that it penetrated the substance and ventricles of the heart. The form of the opening plainly shows that it was most skillfully made, and with an instrument very thin, strong and wide; around this same fissure we perceive traces of fire and combustion."[1]

Many persons suppose the Saint received this celestial favor but once; they are mistaken, St. Teresa's own words are expressly otherwise: "The Lord was pleased that I should have at times a vision of this kind." The human mind is lost in considering the wonderful flights this happy dove, so often wounded, must have made in the regions of Divine Love. We may reasonably believe that these gradual ascensions of Teresa's heart and mind never ceased, but continued with increasing intensity known to God alone. This assertion seems confirmed by the existence in the heart of little holes, apparently the scars of slighter wounds. The above-mentioned physicians made deposition as follows: "We also see in this same heart little round holes, the cause of which we cannot divine. It

---

[1] Life of St. Teresa of Jesus.—*Translation from the Spanish, by Lewis.*

is commonly believed that they are likewise wounds made at different times by the angel's dart."

The little chronicles of the monastery of the Incarnation, expressly declare that this prodigy took place not once only but often, and that the Saint at such times, desired neither to speak nor see, but to be consumed with this sweet suffering. In fact, according to these chronicles, the prodigy continued for many years. She experienced it once when Prioress of the Monastery of the Incarnation. Being in one of the rooms appropriated to the Prioress, and her favorite daughter Anne Maria of Jesus in that above, the latter is alarmed by hearing her sighs and groans, and runs to her assistance, but the Saint dismisses her with these words: "Go, go, my child; I desire only that you may experience the same."

X.

The Breaking of Several Crystal Reliquaries and other Phenomena.

When the Saint's heart was taken from her body, as we shall presently relate in the second part of this book, it was enclosed in a very thin crystal reliquary, through which the faithful could contemplate and venerate it; but very soon this reliquary was found broken. Another having been obtained, in a short time it shared the same fate. This happened several times. Some attributed it to the gases or natural effluvia escaping from the heart, others to a supernatural cause. To prevent a recurrence of the accident, it was judged advisable to pierce little air holes in the upper part of the reliquary; at present they are closed with wax, there being apparently no necessity for keeping them open. These facts have had so many witnesses, that they are beyond doubt.

Father Philip of the Most Holy Trinity, General of the Discalced Carmelites, mentions them in his work on "Mystical Theology," and also in his "Decor Carmeli." It is useless to quote his words here, as they may be found in "St. Teresa's Life," by Father Frederick of St. Anthony, which we have already mentioned. One of the witnesses of the verbal process of 1726, swore that he had seen the broken glass of the reliquary in which the heart had been enclosed, and he had understood, from several very reliable persons, that this fracture was the result of exhalations from the above mentioned heart, which finding no vent, forced their way through the glass. Another affirmed that the heirs of Joseph Gonzalez of Salamanca, preserved as a relic a portion of these crystal fragments. Moreover, Father Stephen of Saints Peter and Paul, former missionary to the Indies and Provincial of the province of Venice, wrote from Rome, January 1, 1752, to his friend and brother in religion, Father Frederick, as follows: "When I saw the heart, I did not perceive that any particle of it was wanting. Subsequently, passing through Logrogno in Navarre, I visited one of our monasteries to see a Sister who was dangerously ill. I then saw upon a little table covered with a cloth, and bearing two lighted tapers, a reliquary containing a relic without name, as well as I can recollect, or proofs of authenticity. The Prioress asked me if, whilst at Alba, I had carefully noticed the Saint's heart, and if it was entire. My answer was an affirmative. She then said, ' and yet the relic you see here is a small particle of the extremity of her heart. Mgr. de Palafox, whilst kissing it from devotion, detached this particle with his teeth. A noble lady became heir to it, and deeming it wrong to keep so precious a treasure concealed, she presented it to our monastery. The identity of the relic was attested by the fact of its breaking the glass of the first reliquary in which it was enclosed: we had to get a new one pierced with three little apertures, and it is thus we have ever since preserved it in our monastery.'"

The fracture of the reliquary containing so

small a portion of the Saint's heart, could not surely have been the result of escaping gases or effluvia; from which we must infer, that neither did the great reliquary enclosing the heart break from causes purely natural. Doubtless, we must avoid multiplying miracles, but why wish to deny them when facts bear such indubitable evidences of the supernatural?

These wonderful exhalations from St. Teresa's heart (due perhaps to a sort of interior effervescence, now ceased,) from that favored tabernacle of the Holy Spirit were also attested by other phenomena. In the verbal process of 1726, there is mention of the little silver dove, a representation of the Holy Spirit, placed above the reliquary containing the heart, and it is affirmed that the lower part of the dove, the only part that could have come in contact with the escaping exhalations, was found blackened, whilst all the rest remained untarnished and bright.

Philip Lopez, in chapter XLIII of the Saint's Life, recounts a wonderful circumstance which was observed in his day. "Although," said he, "any particle whatever of the Saint's flesh exhales a sweet perfume, that of her heart is the sweetest, especially on feast days. This fragrance is then so penetrating that I know not to what it may be compared; and it has the power of communicating itself to all around, so as to overcome the natural perfume of odoriferous objects near.

XI.

Wonderful Apparitions in St. Teresa's Heart.

It really seems as if God intended to glorify, in an especial manner, St. Teresa's heart—that ardent furnace of Divine Love. Listen to another species of prodigy:

Father Emmanuel of St. Jerome, writes as follows in his chronicles of the Order: "Though unworthy, I had the happiness, whilst Assistant Provincial, in 1705, of seeing St. Teresa's Heart at Alba, whither I went to venerate it. And I saw in this heart a perfect image in relief of the Blessed Virgin, holding her Son on her left arm and a golden sceptre in her right hand. My companion, also Assistant Provincial, saw at the same time and in the same heart, an image of our Father, St. Joseph." This occurrence is so frequent that, without ceasing to be marvelous, it commands universal belief.

Those learned theologians, Discalced Carmelites known as the Doctors of Salamanca, render public testimony to this fact. In the second volume of their great work, in the treatise on the Incarnation, when speaking upon the veneration due the relics of Saints, they call Teresa's heart "the wonderful mirror of the Divine Omnipotence, reflecting mysterious images, which are certainly supernatural apparitions."

The glory of this highly-favored creature is manifested by extraordinary apparitions, visible even in the minutest particles of her heart. Father Joseph of Jesus Maria, General of the Order in Spain, had sent, in 1614, to the Carmelite nuns of Puebla in Mexico, a relic of the Saint's heart. Scarcely had it arrived when Mother Elvira of St. Joseph, one of the foundresses of the convent, saw in the relic the image of the Holy Mother, St. Teresa. Her cries of astonishment brought all the other Sisters to the spot, who, at first seeing nothing, began to think it an illusion, when at that moment appeared in the relic a most beautiful image of our Redeemer's face, and then, successively, images of the Eternal Father, of the Most Holy Trinity, of the Blessed Virgin, of the Precursor St. John Baptist, of the Apostle St. Peter, the Prophet Elias and other saints.

One of the most touching, and even painfully vivid of these representations was an *Ecce Homo*, Jesus of Nazareth appearing, indeed, as He was shown to the Jewish people, with streams of crimson blood flowing from His Adorable Head. The religious of Puebla or Angelopolis attested under oath the truth of these apparitions, which were so multiplied eventually that Father Emmanuel says this little relic was called *a window of Heaven*.

We cannot refrain from remarking that similar wonders were reproduced on a very large scale in the relics of St. John of the Cross. No doubt they are attributable to the striking resemblance of this great Saint to the Seraph of Carmel.

Other prodigies not less remarkable have also been noticed in St. Teresa's heart. Sometimes it assumes unusual dimensions. In 1650 the Father-General of the Spanish Carmelites respectfully took the heart in his hands, when suddenly it not only increased to twice its ordinary size, but the Seraphic Mother appeared above it, wearing the habit of Carmel, and so beautiful, so luminous, as to dazzle the eyes of all who beheld the vision. Some were so overcome at the spectacle that they nearly swooned.

XII.

Wonderful History of the Daughter of a Circassian Prince.

Ere finishing an account of the wonders wrought by St. Teresa's heart we will relate the singular event which took place in the life of Teresa Serley, the daughter of a Circassian prince:

She bore at first a pagan name, but at fourteen

years of age renounced the religion of Mahomet, and, under the name of Teresa, she was married to an English nobleman, Robert Scrley. She had been converted to Catholicity by the Discalced Carmelite Fathers of Ispahan, the capital of Persia. Denounced to the Vizier as an apostate from her faith, she was cited to appear before the authorities to answer the charge. Teresa did not refuse to obey, but first wished to fortify herself by receiving the Sacrament of Penance and the Eucharist. For this purpose she sought the Fathers. Encouraged by their exhortations and sustained by Divine grace, she disposed herself for martyrdom. Arrayed in her richest apparel, as if for a grand festival, and accompanied by her servants, she repaired to the place where the judge awaited her. She wore upon her bosom a relic of St. Teresa's heart, which had been given her in Madrid at the instance of the Saint herself, who revealed her wishes to her niece, the venerable Mother Beatrix of Jesus. The heroic Christian declared her intention of suffering every species of torment rather than deny the faith of Jesus Christ. Promises were vain, likewise threats; and, vanquished by her unshaken constancy, the judges at last relinquished the contest, and gave orders that she should be reconducted to her dwelling. The spectators of this touching scene, unable to restrain their admiration, exclaimed aloud: "What a brave woman!" and even the Mahometan priest mingled his praises with theirs.

Having reached home, the servants hastened to take off her rich vestments, that she might rest more comfortably after the great fatigue of the struggle she had just undergone. As she handed the relic of St. Teresa for a moment to one of them, the latter, noticing that it was discolored with blood, thought with her companions, that it must proceed from a wound or hurt their mistress had received during the trial. They carefully examined her, but found not the slightest sign of a wound. Meanwhile the quantity of blood in the reliquary continued to increase, and at length oozed out.

Alarmed beyond measure, they sent in great haste for the Carmelite Fathers. The Superior of the Mission came, accompanied by another member of the Community. Taking the reliquary in his hands, he perceived in the relic of the heart seven tiny wounds, from each of which flowed a slender stream of blood. At this discovery the religious themselves were seized with awe, and acknowledging the truth of the prodigy, were unable to restrain their tears. It is not easy to discover what St. Teresa wished to express by this miracle. Some thought it signified her ardent desire of martyrdom, others, the rescinblance of her heart to Mary's transfixed by the Seven Dolors, so that the heart of this incomparable woman bore not only a striking likeness to that of Jesus, but also to that of His Mother. After a little while, in the presence of all, the blood ceased flowing, and the countess, having had collected that which issued from the reliquary, presented it to the Discalced Carmelite Fathers established in Rome at the Convent of Santa Maria della Scala.

Teresa Serley died at Rome in the year 1688.

SECOND PART.

Recent Wonders of St. Teresa's Heart.

I.

Recent Publication of a Spanish Pamphlet on the Subject.

The Rev. Nemesius Cardellach, a Lazarist priest residing at Badajoz, Spain, published in 1876 at Valencia a pamphlet, which we had the pleasure of reading a few years ago. It is entitled, "St. Teresa of Jesus and the Thorns of her Heart, venerated in the Monastery of the Discalced Carmelites at Alba de Tormes, Diocese of Salamanca." The object of this little book is to diffuse a knowledge of the more recent wonders which St. Teresa's heart, for a number of years past, has offered to the consideration of all who come to venerate it.

Written with great simplicity, it shows that the author possessed the true spirit of inquiry. On receiving the necessary permissions, he repaired to the spot, saw for himself, and carefully collected the most minute information possible. The ecclesiastical authority of Valencia, ere allowing him to publish his book, submitted it to a very severe examination, inasmuch as it treated of miraculous matters, upon the nature and truth of which the Church, that alone has the right to decide, had not yet given judgment. Finding everything therein in accordance with the rules of prudence and canonical law, the Cardinal Archbishop of Valencia gave it his approbation, which the author prefixed to the work.

We have every reason then, to feel proud of this author and his work presented to us under such favorable auspices. However, knowing that the Court of Rome holds under examination the series of facts we are about to consider, we shall stretch our prudence to the utmost limits and refrain from expressing our own opinion, contenting ourselves with merely recounting a well-authenticated fact, in regard to which there is, and can be, no doubt. This fact, or rather series of facts, we shall designate by the word *wonders*, without pronouncing upon the question as to whether they belong to the natural order, as some think, or the supernatural, as the majority suppose. It may have been God's will to glorify St. Teresa's heart by a natural wonder, for He derives His glory as well from wonders of nature as from those that surpass it.

II.

Author's Prologue.

The entire translation of this Spanish pamphlet not appearing to us altogether advisable, we shall content ourselves with making long extracts from it, scrupulously adhering to the substance and meaning of the original. We give below a portion of the prologue:

"The thorns of St. Teresa's heart! This is certainly a wonderful thing, a phenomenon unique of its kind and claiming our especial attention. Thorns or objects resembling them, which have sprung forth, increased, developed, and are preserved, or rather reproduced, for the long space of forty years (1836-1875), and that in a dry, arid heart deprived of all the necessary conditions of life! Who could refrain from astonishment at such a prodigy? The echo of this marvel has resounded, not only beyond the narrow limits of Alba de Tormes and the Diocese of Salamanca, but even those of Spain; it has filled all Europe, and is now heard at the extremities of the earth.

"A fact so wonderful has elicited divers opinions, some physicians believing it a miracle, and others denying it all claim to the supernatural. These conflicting sentiments are now before the public, and they have very forcibly impressed me with increased devotion for St. Teresa.

"And how could I remain indifferent when there is question of God's glory and the Saint's honor? Within the sanctuary of my heart I could not doubt the divine intervention in these productions inexplicable to science. I have submitted a knowledge of them in two inquiries to the ecclesiastical tribunal. But since they are already known, and have given rise to contradictory opinions, the solution of which will increase God's glory and the Saint's honor, I have believed it my duty to present, in its entirety, all that has been said upon the subject so as to fix it, if possible, in a clear light and in such a manner as may afford a foundation more or less solid, whenever the subject should be mooted.

"The idea of forestalling the Church's judgment has never entered my mind. In matters of Faith, morals and discipline, there is no other authority, and I recognize none save that of the Catholic, Apostolic and Roman Church, to which I have the happiness of belonging, in whose bosom I desire to live and die, and to whose authority I submit unreservedly. And, moreover, if in the course of my work I say something touching the marvelous nature of the fact, using even the word *miracle*, I here state that I am expressing merely my individual opinion, the result, in a measure, of the premises I am going to lay down and establish. Consequently, to these and similar expressions must be attributed no more weight and character, than to those of a private opinion based upon facts previously mentioned."

After other considerations as to the plan of his book and its high spiritual aim, the author continues:

"It does not treat of an isolated, transitory occurrence in regard to which illusion is possible on the part of a witness, neither of a favor obtained by some pious means calculated to win graces and favors, nor of a vision or spiritual manifestation in which the enemy of souls, self-love, or a vivid and fertile imagination could play an important part; no, it is nothing of this. On the contrary, it treats of a material, abiding, visible, palpable thing, which for the space of forty years spontaneously sprang into existence, increased, developed, sustained life and multiplied in the sight of all the world; of a well-known fact, which every one who comes to Alba de Tormes can see for himself—a fact upon which the ecclesiastical authority, conformably to orders from Rome, has opened an investigation, upon which four doctors of medicine, surgery and pharmacy have passed judgment—a fact, in fine, that I myself (for which a thousand thanks to our Lord!) have had occasion to examine most carefully, and relative to which I have, at two different times, communicated desirable private information to his illustrious Lordship who deigned to receive it, and even inserted it in the verbal process. It treats of a fact controverted indeed, but because there were contrary opinions regarding it, some believing it a miracle, others not; of a fact already exercising public attention, and become a constant theme of conversations, eliciting many affirmations on one side and negations on the other; of a fact certain in itself since its existence no one can deny, but uncertain as to its cause which, in spite of obstacles, I shall endeavor to ascertain and prove if possible. It treats of a reality visible and palpable, but of an undefined nature, concerning which it behooves us to inquire; it treats, in fine, of solving the mystery (to science) of the thorns seen in the crystal globe enclosing the blessed heart of St. Teresa, of attempting to establish something positive against the negations of certain physicians, the reports from ignorance or malice circulated among the people, and even against the hypothetical objections presented to me on the subject."

The author concludes his prologue by inviting every one to visit Alba, and examine for himself these marvels the Lord has wrought.

III.

The Rev. N. Cardellach at Albà de Tormes.

To give an idea of the confidence that may be placed in this pious missionary's words and testimony on the subject, we deem it advisable to present here an abridgment of the introduction following his prologue. Whilst at Madrid and visiting the Spanish provinces, he frequently heard of the thorns of St. Teresa's heart. In November, 1873, he received orders from his Superior to conduct a retreat for the two houses of the Daughters of Charity in Salamanca. And there more than ever did he hear on the subject. Don Thomas Bellestra, Archdeacon of the Cathedral, and several other very worthy priests made especial mention of it to him. However, they did not conceal the objection of certain doctors to its miraculous nature, and particularly that of a distinguished Jesuit skilled in the natural sciences. "After hearing these various statements," says he, " my heart was impressed with the idea that there must be something mysterious and supernatural in the matter," and he expressed himself thus to the Bishop of Salamanca, Mgr. Joachim Lluch Garriga, subsequently transferred to the See of Barcelona in Catalonia. The latter told him of the arguments of the opposing party, the orders from Rome to have a canonical investigation, and his own earnest desire to see the matter settled. In hearing all this, especially the diversity of opinion, Father Cardellach, for want of a firm standpoint, could arrive at no definite conclusion, but his heart was strongly biased in favor of the supernatural origin of the prodigy.

Some time after, the Daughters of Charity were entrusted with the charge of a hospital at Alba de Tormes, and he profited by this circumstance to repair to the place. Four Sisters, the above-named Archdeacon, and Don Ferdinand Iglesias, another priest, accompanied him. We can readily imagine Father Cardellach's joy at seeing, for the first time, though only a few minutes, the heart of St. Teresa. The good priest believed it his duty to communicate to the prelate his humble opinion concerning this extraordinary relic, and his words inspired such confidence that the latter enjoined upon him the writing of a detailed account of the visit, which injunction was readily complied with and the narrations soon put into the Bishop's hands.

From this time till the early part of January, 1875, more than a year later, the missionary heard nothing farther on the subject. It was then he again went to Salamanca to conduct a retreat for the Daughters of Charity there, and their sisters who came from Alba de Tormes to take part in it. The latter urged him to return to Alba and make a more leisurely, careful examination of the Saint's heart. To their entreaties were joined those of the Archdeacon, other priests and laymen. They told him that his narration had been the only one of importance; the only one calculated to throw the least light upon so delicate a subject; that it was indeed the very soul of the canonical investigation. But he could not be prevailed upon to go. God's hour, though very near, had not come.

The Bishop of Salamanca, having been transferred to Barcelona, was succeeded by Mgr. Narcisse Martinez Izquierdo. In 1875, on the occasion of the jubilee granted by Pope Pius IX, this prelate, wishing to have a mission given in every parish of his diocese, called upon the Lazarists for this purpose. Among the laborers sent into the evangelical field in answer to his call, was the Rev. M. Cardellach, who, by the Bishop's orders and without any preconceived design, commenced the missions at Alba de Tormes. Whilst here the good missionary whose heart, according to his own expression, "had become identified with that of St. Teresa," obtained the Bishop's permission, under date of April 26, 1875, to enter the monastery and cell, so as to examine most carefully (though with all due veneration), the heart of the holy Reformatrix.

On the 29th of April, to his great joy, he penetrated the enclosure of the monastery. The date was for him one of sad and terrible memory, for on the 29th of April, 1857, he had been taken prisoner by General Garcia Pueblita, at Michoacan, Mexico, and kept in a dungeon three days, hourly expecting to be brought forth only to be shot. The confessor and chaplain of the Carmelites accompanied him to the monastery, and both were conducted to the little chamber where is enshrined the heart of St. Teresa, who died here in the year 1582, as we have already stated. After several visits the good priest, deeply impressed with what he had seen, could not restrain his unbounded admiration for the sanctity of this great woman, and the infinite grandeur of Him who created her; he ceased not to proclaim the praises of God in these magnificent, incomprehensible works of his hand. He then resolved to write out his reflections at length (though without exceeding due limit), and present them to the prelate. The principal subject of his work was *the thorns*, but, as he tells us himself, urged by a very strong impulse of grace, he could not forbear dwelling upon the wound, *so like that in the heart of Jesus*. This impulse led him to give, in his work, an abridged life of the Saint, that Saint who, as he says on the eighteenth page of his work, was one of the four persons raised up by God in His Church to reform morals; the other three being, in his opinion, Ignatius of Loyola, Vincent de Paul, and Alphonsus Ligouri, the honor of the three principal Catholic nations.[1]

His task accomplished, he had a conversation with the Bishop. On returning to Madrid he showed the *fac simile* of the Saint's heart to a venerable priest, and gave him a detailed account of these wonders. It was then for the first time he realized all the difficulties of the subject. He resolved to solve them, and believing his efforts successful, communicated the details to this ecclesiastic, whose replies, in the shape of objections, vigorous and striking, increased the gravity of the question. He now applied himself solely to these, and answered them to his own satisfaction, for which he returned thanks to Holy Mother Teresa.

Father Cardellach says that his work is imperfect, and much less carefully put together than he desired, but pleads in apology the pressing occupations of the ministry, which left him very

---

[1] The author could likewise have mentioned the holy Archbishop of Milan, Cardinal Charles Borromeo, so justly called the Council of Trent incarnate. His death took place in 1584, just two years after St. Teresa's.

little time at his own disposal. "However," he continues, "I have presented the fact and given the explanation which, in my opinion, was most reasonable and accurate. I have solved difficulties more or less plausible, I have done away with objections, and in every respect, as far as I can judge, I have proceeded logically, offering to the reader's attention premises which prepare the way for the legitimate consequences drawn from them."

This introduction is dated Sunday, September 19th, 1875, Feast of the Seven Dolors of Our Lady.

IV.

Description of the Anterior of St. Teresa's Heart.

Father Cardellach, between his prologue and introduction, has inserted two lithographs, a work carefully executed by the skillful Valero. They represent in their real size at present the anterior and posterior views of St. Teresa's heart, contained in a heart-shaped crystal reliquary. We shall give an exact description of them in this and the following chapter.

At the top of the crystal is a golden lid, enameled, circular in form, and surmounted by ball-shaped ornaments. In it are ten respiratory holes, now closed with wax, but formerly open, to allow passage to the effluvia from the heart, which effluvia, in the opinion of some, caused the fracture of the reliquary. The inner sides of the crystal globe are sprinkled with a dust, of which we shall speak hereafter. The heart is held suspended by three brass wires, fastened to the lid, and crossing one another under the lower extremity of the sacred organ. In the upper part of the heart, and on the left of the spectator, one sees nearly the whole of the great wound made by the Seraph with his burning dart. We say nearly the whole, because, on turning from right to left of the spectator, the extremity of the wound is seen in the posterior part. This has caused some of the authors, already quoted, to say that the Seraph's dart went through and through the heart of St. Teresa, but it does not appear so to us. A little cross, apparently an expansion of the wound, is immediately above it, thus finishing the wonderful resemblance of the Saint's heart to that of Jesus.

Just below the extremity of the wound, and on the right of the spectator, we perceive a small dark spot, heart-shaped, and resembling a brilliant or gem, azure-colored and violet. Still farther down, and to the right of the spectator, we distinguish black spots, like tobacco leaves when prepared for use. Beneath these, nearer the middle of the heart and to the left, is a collection of little grains, a species of white stones that one might easily suppose were pearls or grains of sand. Yet lower, and still on the left, is another wound (though a small one) made by the Seraph. On the right, we perceive protuberances, reminding one of little stones pricked in various places. In regard to these, we will remark that they are formed by the skin or membrane enveloping the whole heart, and Father Cardellach describes them as very rough.

Finally, yet farther down, are the famous thorns and other excrescences. These bear no resemblance to one another, either in shape, length or the direction they take. One, on the right of the spectator, has the appearance of a little branch, and, according to Father Cardellach, it springs directly from the heart. A second, on the other side, resembles a piece of crooked wire, terminating in a point. It is very slender, and near its base we see another object, apparently not developed, but showing a tendency to ascend parallel with the latter. In the neighborhood of this little branch is a slender wire or curved stem, growing horizontally from the heart. These three objects bear no resemblance to thorns. They are designated in our engraving by numbers 15, 16 and 17. Number 18, on the contrary, at least in shape, is an exact thorn, with a sharp point. The author styles it *the great thorn*. Number 19 is another thorn. It has no point, and arises parallel with the crystal. Number 20 denotes an excrescence at the base of the heart, resembling shreds of wool or worsted; number 21, a third little thorn, with two points at the top; number 22, an abundant deposit of dust or sediment at the bottom of the crystal; number 23, the spot whence these thorns seem to arise; number 24, the inner and lower part of the crystal globe; and—lastly, number 25—on the right of the spectator, five little thorns, of different sizes and growing in different directions. They apparently spring from the dust. We have now seen that the anterior portion of the heart, with the interior of the crystal, offers to our consideration two large thorns, properly so designated in regard to form, one having a point, the other not; a third thorn, very much smaller and forked at the top; then a fourth, fifth, sixth, seventh and eighth, more like little lances or threads than thorns.

Such is the aspect of the first lithograph by Valero. Let us pass to the second.

V.

Description of the Posterior Portion. The Second Lithograph Presents the Opposite Side of St. Teresa's Heart.

In the upper part, on the right of the spectator, is seen a slight portion of the other extremity of the wound. A little below and more to the left, is a cavity produced apparently by the abstraction of a piece of the heart. Still farther to the left are numbers of little pricks, or very small, separate wounds, probably made by the Seraph's dart. We also perceive three others much larger, due to the same cause, two almost in the centre of the heart, and a third at its lower extremity. The whole surface of the heart is shaggy, and according to the author's expression, it looks as if enveloped in tiny radicles of ivy. The great pointed thorn which in this second picture is seen from another side, presents near its base, a point arising from it in a horizontal line. Two long, slender thorns, parallel and inclined, more like lances or lines, now strike our attention; then another little lance or pointed excrescence arising from the base of the great thorn, and itself thorn-shaped. Again we notice two short lances, parallel and perpendicular. To the left of these, is a little

62   THE WONDERS OF THE

branch like that described in the preceding chapter, and likewise springing from the lower extremity of the great pointed thorn. And finally, one remarks a black segment or small object, also arising from the base of the great pointed thorn and curved.

Thus we see that this great pointed thorn is in every respect most singular: first, because it has the shape of a veritable thorn; secondly, because at the side of its base there arises another veritable thorn; thirdly, because from the bottom issue conjointly, a small thorn designated as number 22 in the lithograph, a little branch number 26, and a black segment number 28. This second lithograph needs no further explanation, everything else being similar to that of the first. We shall minutely describe each object.

VI.

Traditions Collected on the Spot by Father Cardellach Relating to the Abstraction of St. Teresa's Heart.

Before giving a description of the various objects mentioned in our last chapter, we must acquaint our readers with the traditions relative to the abstraction of St. Teresa's heart, (traditions collected on the spot by the good missionary), which very audacious and, to human appearances, unjustifiable act, was the work of a lay Sister. We shall give the account as near as possible in his own words.

The Saint's body had been entrusted to her daughters of the monastery of the Incarnation at Alba de Tormes. As may be supposed they held it in great veneration, and were ever fearful lest some day so holy a treasure should be taken from them. Influenced by this feeling, a lay Sister provides herself with a knife, and unknown to the Community approaches the sacred remains. With more love than skill she opens the Saint's virginal bosom and draws forth as well as she can, the heart. Placing it between two wooden vessels, she takes it to her cell. Immediately the whole monastery was filled with a celestial odor, and the religious ran to the spot where their inestimable relic was kept. They discovered the perpetrator of the deed, by drops of fresh blood all along the path she had taken in carrying the holy Mother's heart to the cell.

Horrified at what was now beyond repair, they immediately informed the Superiors of the Order, who strongly censured the Sister's temerity. It is said that a penance was imposed upon her, and she was sent to another convent. Our author attributes her act to a special impulse of the Holy Spirit. Be that as it may, it is certain that the good Sister accepted the correction with humility and patience. According to the traditions of the monastery, two others lent their hand to the work, for there are preserved the names of three transferred to another monastery by way of penance, two lay Sisters, Sisters Catherine Baptista de Pedrahita and Maria of St. Albert of Alba, and a choir Sister, Sister Inez of the Cross. Their Superiors, in sending them to a convent whose name is not given, wished thus to avoid all investigation or inquiry on the subject, as appears from some notes in their "Book of Professions."

The abstraction of this blessed heart must have taken place between the years 1586 and 1588. The Saint's body was restored to Alba in 1586, and after some relics were taken from it, in the year 1588, it was placed in the shrine, locked by three keys, whence Father Cardellach justly concludes, that the Sister's bold deed necessarily occurred between these dates. According to tradition, the good Sister feared a second translation of the Saint's body from their monastery, and determined to secure for her own Community the possession of the most precious relic of all—the heart.

It was immediately placed in a crystal case,

several of which were successively broken, as we have already mentioned. According to our author, the cause of this has never been discovered, but he says it might very reasonably be attributed to the influence of the heart itself, or an abundance of gases escaping from it. On the 15th of October, 1760, the last translation of the Saint's body took place. On this occasion, the heart was enshrined in the beautiful and costly reliquary (the gift of an Italian prince) in which it is shown at the present day. Since that epoch, both it and the Saint's arm are kept in the turn at the Epistle side of the main altar, the turn communicating with a little chamber on the ground floor of the monastery; and it is there these relics are exposed to the veneration of the faithful. Before this translation they were venerated in the sacristy turn.[1]

The crystal heart enclosing St. Teresa's is seven fingers and a quarter in length, five and three quarters wide. The lid is gold-enameled, with rubies. Around it are the little holes of which

---

[1] Cloistered religious communicate with externs through the medium of the turn, which is found in all monasteries. The turn here spoken of is a special one constructed for the reliquaries, in order that the religious may possess these precious relics within their cloister, and yet may be able, on certain occasions, to expose them to the veneration of the faithful, without any violation of enclosure.

we have spoken, now closed with wax. They are large enough to admit a very big needle. Above, cast in silver, is a representation of the Holy Spirit, and back of this, sun rays of gilded silver. The bottom is also silver, with cast ornaments of enameled gold, and encircled by three rows of rubies. Its height is four fingers and a quarter. It is screwed upon a silver pedestal, which supports the whole reliquary. This reliquary, in the shape of an arch, is likewise of silver with gilded ornaments, the heads of cherubim and angels, one of them bearing the inscription, *Teresa of Jesus*, another *Jesus of Teresa*. The design is in the Roman style. We shall not attempt any minute description, but content ourselves with mentioning that the artist has surmounted it by a representation of the Transverberation of the Saint's Heart, than which nothing could be more appropriate.

VII.

The Examination of the Heart of St. Teresa.

On the 29th of April, 1875, at 8 o'clock in the morning, Father Cardellach, with the Father Sanctos del Carmelo y Salcedo, Confessor and Chaplain to the House, penetrated the enclosure of the monastery. Near the window of the little chamber, the religious had placed a table covered with a cloth. The Reverend Mother opened the door and grate of the turn enclosing the Saint's heart and arm. The Confessor placed the first-named relic upon the table. Father Cardellach knelt, adored God in His Saint, implored His grace and assistance, and, recommending himself to the Seraph of Carmel, proceeded to the examination of the heart. He was deeply impressed, but nevertheless, not to such a degree as to bias his judgment in the slightest, or prevent his attention being fixed upon the work before him. The five or six visits he made this inestimable relic, were in all respects similar to the first, except that he remained alone, so as the more easily to prolong his happy study.

He turned and re-turned the Saint's heart; he examined it from the front, the sides, the back; by the natural light of day, by an artificial light, lifting the heart so as to view it from below, and again lowering it, that he might look down upon it. Sometimes he used the pale light of a taper, sometimes little mirrors; again a microscope or very powerful lenses. Often he would place one glass upon another—a smaller upon a greater—spending thus at each visit from three to four hours. He could not tear himself away from this sacred spot. So strongly was his heart united to St. Teresa's that, had not duty called him elsewhere, he had willingly remained forever.

As there was not sufficient light from the window near which the table had been placed, he moved the reliquary to another window, looking towards the interior of the monastery and out upon the country. He did this in all subsequent visits, being thus better enabled to note the characteristics of the holy relic. Everything in this heart appeared worthy of remark—its color, its size, its preservation without any species of embalming, the wounds, the thorns, the radicles, the dust. Every day something new excited his attention, and caused him to elevate his soul to the Sovereign Dispenser of good.

The length of the heart is about four inches, its width in the upper part, or auricles, two inches, and in the lower half an inch. In viewing it as it rested in the Seraphic Mother's bosom, the point would be turned to the left and the wound on the right. According to Father Cardellach, it baffled description. Its general aspect is that of a heart flattened and irregularly contracted. It is fleshless, dry, shrunken, and under the wound in the posterior part, on the spectator's right, there has been for a long time a cavity, quite a piece having been taken out lengthwise. We must remark that this cavity is also covered with that wrinkled, yellowish

membrane, enveloping nearly the whole organ;
it is here united and continuous, in other parts
like a sort of net, permitting one at certain
intervals to perceive the natural color of the
heart. This pellicle or membrane which presents
many wrinkles and interruptions, has, he says,
a disagreeable aspect. From it stand out fibrous
or thread-like particles, which at first sight
remind one of little radicles of ivy.

In the intermediary places or interruptions,
and especially near the wound, are seen several
great black spots, much more perceptible in
front. This should not excite very much surprise, since the Spouse of the Canticles exclaims:
"I am black but beautiful. Do not consider
me that I am brown, because the sun hath
altered my color." Almost directly under the
centre of the wound, they appear as a band the
color of blood, nearly the fifth of an inch wide, and
from four-fifths of an inch to over an inch long.
It has ramifications, and something similar is
seen under the lower lip of the wound and in
other places. At certain points these spots are
not so dark, but more like the natural color of
the organ.

Over the whole surface of the heart, we notice
scattered here and there, little shreds of the pellicle or membrane, dry, shrivelled, very adherent,
and presenting an irregular, indescribable aspect.

These rugged places of a yellowish white, together with the black, gray and bloody spots, the little stones and the abundance of rootlets arising from every part, give to the heart a most peculiar appearance, which, according to our author, cannot fail to excite great astonishment, especially when we consider the wound and the thorns. It forms a collection of inexplicable mysteries, a sort of microscopic world, that our Lord offers to the piety of the faithful and the discussion of the learned.

VIII.

The Color, Protuberances, Grains or Little Stones, and Spots of Blood of St. Teresa's Heart.

At first sight, the color of this precious relic appears to be a light chestnut (due, no doubt, in a great measure to the inequalities of the yellowish membrane we have already described), but in observing it more closely, we perceive different colors united, one very distinct from another; consequently, the tint is indescribable, and it would be as difficult to give an exact idea of it, as to paint with one stroke of the pencil, the earth and its varied hues as seen from an elevation.

We shall say a few words more in regard to these protuberances or inequalities. They proceed from the skin that covers the surface, or the fibrous membrane which probably enveloped the heart; in drying, it contracted and tore in some places, thus producing that rough, disagreeable aspect of which we have spoken. By its numberless holes it resembles in certain parts a net or sieve. The broken, detached fibres standing forth, have the appearance of roots with their radicles, tiny stems, or plants, for which we have no name.

We have said that the skin probably enveloped the heart. But we have also mentioned the abstraction of quite a good-sized piece of this organ in the posterior part, lengthwise, and back of the wound; yet the cavity thus produced is entirely covered by this skin. This circumstance has caused some doubts in the author's mind, and partially suspended his judgment. The portion of membrane covering the cavity is exactly of the same color, nature and appearance as in other parts. The question arises, how could this be? Who presided at the operation? What was the object of it? "I candidly acknowledge," says Father Cardellach, "that it is a mystery to me."

Over the whole surface of this blessed heart, we notice, either in groups or isolated, little white points like tiny stones or grains of rice. Some of them are sparkling, and, seen through a magnifying glass, resemble the grains of sand on the banks of a river. Some are larger, some smaller; some are whiter, more polished, and inserted in a more regular manner than others, thus reminding one of the fibrous membrane by their variety. Two or three collected, somewhat wide and flat, placed under and a little distance from the lower lip of the wound, at its extremity on the right, claim especial attention. They are the color of a gem—deep azure and violet. According to a revelation our holy Mother made a religious, these stones or grains represent the virtues with which her heart was adorned; and there is even a little exercise of piety in honor of them practiced for ten days. To us these seeming stones recall the words the Church places in the mouth of St. Agnes, virgin and martyr: *"He has surrounded me with pearls, precious and brilliant."* And these pearls can be no other than the holy Mother's virtues.

Among the spots, we notice one more than an inch in length, and about one-fifth of an inch wide. It is formed of rays, some of them a deep red, others a blackish color, which gradually vanish as they extend from the centre of the heart to its lower extremity. It is a spot of blood. Below the whole extent of the wound's lower lip, and especially from this radiating spot to the right extremity of the wound, we perceive the same traces of blood, but a little more deeply colored.

IX.

Description of the Great and Little Wounds of St. Teresa's Heart.

According to St. Teresa, the Seraph who pierced her with his dart stood on the left. Nevertheless, he plunged the dart from right to left of her heart, as can be plainly seen in the picture. The wound, or Transverberation, is in the upper and widest part of the heart, in a horizontal line on the right side, and is at least two inches long. We cannot, indeed, understand this, or reconcile the holy Mother's words with the evidence of the wound itself, plainly showing that the hand which inflicted it must have been from the right and not the left side. Father Cardellach, perhaps noticing this discrepancy, as well as ourselves, writes as follows, we know not upon what authority: "The Seraph, leaning back of Teresa, towards her right hand, plunged the dart in the anterior part." So, according to this, the angel stood on her left, and leaned back of her in such a way that the dart wounded her in the right side of the heart.

We really do not understand this; it is incomprehensible. However, we must bear in mind that although the angel was real, and the wound he inflicted real, the arrow was not, but only represented to the Saint's imagination. Consequently, there is nothing astonishing if the angel, that in her vision stood on her left, opened the wound in the right side of her heart. It is also possible, that the Saint during her whole life never knew on which side the wound was. Good common sense teaches us, that there is necessarily no physical connection between a real wound and a dart, which exists only in imagination. We say, *which exists only in imagination,* because the holy Mother affirmed that she never had corporeal visions, striking the exterior senses. Such is our explanation, let others produce a better.

The wound does not appear of equal size throughout its extent, but on the right side of the heart, that is, on the left of the spectator, is the widest aperture, gradually diminishing until it terminates on the other side in a curved point. The spectator, who directly faces it, cannot embrace the whole extent of the wound, which, as we have said, beginning at the right of the sacred organ, ends in a point on the other side. This has led certain reliable authors, and some persons who have seen the heart, to state that the angelic dart pierced through and through, which, in our opinion, does not seem to be the fact. In the upper lip of the wound and very near the centre, is a cleft, which, if the lithograper Valero has depicted correctly, is in the form of a cross, thus forming another strong point of resemblance between Teresa's heart and that of Jesus. We do not know why Father Cardellach failed to mention this peculiarity in his narration, for it struck our eye immediately.

All along the edges of the wound we perceive traces of a burn or cauterization, especially in the two rents of the upper lip, forming a cross. One might suppose it burned by an incandescent coal or red hot iron. Several other authors had already mentioned this circumstance. The evidences prove that the substance and ventricles of the heart, were pierced by a thin, sharp, broad instrument. It must have reached the centre of the heart as regards breadth, and even further, but did not go through. Yet Teresa of Jesus, who received the wound in 1559, lived till the early part of October, twenty-three years longer! A much lighter wound must infallibly have caused instantaneous death! O prodigy of the hand of God!

We come now to the little wounds. They were observed in the last century, by certain doctors of medicine and surgeons called upon to make deposition, on the occasion of the process for the confirmation of the miracle of the Transverberation. In their exclusively scientific narration they declared, that besides the wound, which was the principal object of their investigation, they had noticed, both in the anterior and posterior portions of the heart, little wounds for which they could not account. Our indefatigable Missionary made them an especial subject of observation. He found four. One is in the right side of the heart (the left of the spectator), just below the centre. It is seen by having the heart directly opposite. Two others are in the posterior portion near the centre, distant from each other about one-tenth of an inch, and the upper one being three times larger than the lower. A fourth is found in the curved end of the heart; it is one-fifth of an inch from the extremity, being thus, as it were, a central point. These holes or wounds are from one-twenty-fifth to one-twelfth of an inch deep, and partly concealed by the yellowish fibrous membrane, enwrapping the whole heart as a vestment.

Besides these we perceive in the posterior portion others resembling pin pricks, almost opposite the right extremity of the great wound, and probably due to the same cause. The protuberances and inequalities of the skin prevent their being carefully examined.

Father Cardellach, after as careful an examination as circumstances would permit, declared that they were produced by the Seraph's dart, for they likewise bear marks of having been burned. But why are these holes round? He gives four mystical reasons, which we believe it our duty to pass over in silence. And, indeed, a divine or miraculous work cannot be subject to any law ordinary or extraordinary, it being far from easy to give the why and the wherefore. However, we will not say that the good Missionary's reflections and opinion on this point, are unworthy of consideration.

X.

The Deposit of Dust Under the Heart.

Here is another marvel, though of a different nature. At the bottom of the crystal containing St. Teresa's blessed heart, is a deposit of dust weighing half an ounce, or, at the most, an ounce. According to several medical experts, it might have been formed by the accumulation of infinite particles of the heart's exterior envelope crumbling away. They also thought it might be ordinary dust, which had penetrated the apertures of the coverlid before they were closed. Don Jose Estevan Laurent, Don

Emmanuel Eléna Alfonso, Don Dominique Sanchez Lopez and Don Angelo Villar y Macias, all doctors, signed a paper declaring it the residuum from the natural drying up of the heart for three centuries.

It presents an irregular appearance, not forming a plane surface, but being in heaps and in a much greater quantity on the right than the left of the spectator facing the heart. Although it does not prevent our examining this organ, the radicles and the thorns, yet it interferes with our seeing distinctly and ascertaining whence the phenomenal objects spring. We cannot, indeed, discover whether they have their origin in the dust (an opinion our author deems improbable), or whether they come directly from the heart, which he thinks beyond doubt, although they push their way through the dust on opposite sides.

The supposition that this is ordinary dust, which, from time to time, found its way through the respiratory apertures, is inadmissible. Even if a little had penetrated these openings, it must have been in such small quantities, as when collected after the course of years, could have amounted to a very slight heap at most. But the testimony of the nuns decides this question most conclusively. They affirm that in 1836, before the first appearance of the thorns, there was no dust. The respiratory holes were at that time closed with wax, and this covered with a small piece of colored cloth. In 1875, no religious in the house remembered the closing of these apertures.

On the 25th of January, 1726, two doctors of medicine, Don Blasius Perez de Villaharta and Don Emmanuel de Robles, made this observation: "In the bottom of the crystal we perceive a very thin vapor, or obscurity of the glass, caused, no doubt, by the gases which, escaping from the lower part of the heart, find no vent." This obscuration, then, had already been observed, and attributed to the effluvia of the heart, but there was no allusion to the deposit of dust, the thorns, the threads, or any of the phenomena we have mentioned. What, then, could be the origin of this dust? How was it formed? The question appears so much the more inexplicable, as physicians tell us, that the heart is dried up, mummified, incorrupt.

Could it be the outer envelopes of the heart crumbling away from time? The author says he will not positively deny this, for it is possible. However, he adds that the dark part of the heart, to which this dust corresponds in color, is smooth and compact, showing no signs of dissolution nor the slightest tendency to crumble. The fibrous or shriveled membrane covering nearly the whole surface of the heart is torn in different places, and rises in points, reminding one of little roots or particles snatched in two, exactly like flesh that one had tried to strip from the bones. The molecules when detached, had they formed a deposit at the bottom of the vase, would not have looked like dust, nor would they have been of the same color as this residuum; for the outer, wrinkled tegument is of a tawny white. We must consequently attribute the dust to some other reason, than the giving way of the cardiac envelope.

Father Cardellach believes the real origin of the dust to be as follows: " From the surface of the heart," says he, " arose exhalations, which, finding no vent, obscured the sides of the glass. In the course of years these vapors, becoming denser and heavier, fell of their own weight to the bottom of the crystal, and there collected in little heaps. This conjecture appears certain from present evidences. The inner walls of the glass are so impregnated with this dust that in certain places, especially on the side of the great pointless thorn, it forms masses almost as large as a grain of wheat. If this matter comes from the Saint's heart, why does it not fall perpendicularly to the very bottom of the vase and remain there? Why should it escape in a direction somewhat horizontal, when there is no wind to agitate it or to hinder the fall? Hence, we must conclude that it is not composed of detached particles, fallen from the heart, but of emanations which, diffused over the inner surface of the glass, deposit themselves upon the sides, to which they adhere, until either from their own weight, or shaken by the jarring of the turn or moving of the reliquary, they collect and form in the lower part of the vase such heaps as those, that now hinder a minute examination of the extremity of the heart."

This explanation of its origin, heretofore unknown, may be true, but it presents grave difficulties which should be removed ere it can command implicit belief. The origin of the dust, we say, is of recent date. It appeared after the thorns; the emanations of the heart, on the contrary, belonged to a much earlier period, and had ceased before the appearance of the thorns and dust, so that the apertures made for their passage have long been closed. How, then, can any one talk of these emanations as if still affecting the surroundings of the heart? And in years past, when really escaping, why did they produce no other effect than a slight obscuration of the glass? These are questions which we, who have not been on the spot, find it impossible to answer. Moreover, we must remember that the fracture of the crystal was attributed to the strength of these imprisoned effluvia, an explanation very doubtful in our opinion, as the smallest relics of the heart produced the same effect. But admitting the truth of this explanation, how is it that the present emanations do not break the glass?

"Around the lower extremity of the heart," says Father Cardellach, "in front, on the sides, and below, we perceive a species of dust, altogether different in color and appearance from the former. It resembles grains of rice, very dark and half ground." He frankly declares his ignorance of its origin, but is inclined to believe it proceeds from emanations at the bottom of the heart, and not from the lateral surfaces. And precisely from this spot the thorns appear to spring.

Over the surface of this dust, and mingled with it, are little grains of different sizes and colors—black, dark, whitish—resembling the grains encrusted upon the heart itself.

As the famous thorns were the principal objects of Father Cardellach's observation, and this dust prevented his ascertaining whence they sprung, he bethought himself of repeated light blows on the outside of the crystal, hoping thus to level the masses of dust. With the ends of his fingers he struck the empty side of the glass, so as to bring to that spot the dust heaped up on the other side, and thus obtain a good view of the lower extremity of the heart, and assure himself of the exact spot whence the thorns issued. He effected a partial leveling of the dust, but not sufficient for him to bring his researches to a successful issue; there was always a point open to doubt, which however did not weaken his well-grounded conjectures, that from the extremity of the heart, concealed by this dust, the thorns arise, branching off in different directions.

XI.

Our Opinion upon the Dust, the Little Heaps of Whitish Threads and Tufts of Wool.

In holding always to our firm resolution, of not declaring, even as an individual opinion, that the facts concerning St. Teresa's heart are miraculous, ere the ecclesiastical authority, the only competent judge in such matters, shall have decided, we will nevertheless venture to say, that the deposit of dust under our holy Mother's heart is truly wonderful, and baffles human science. It is one thing to call a fact miraculous, or above all the laws of nature, and another to say, that it is wonderful, or surpasses man's present knowledge of nature's secrets. Numberless phenomena, even the most ordinary, whilst not beyond natural laws, are certainly wonderful, and have so far eluded the human understanding, such as earthquakes, hail, universal gravitation, etc. In regard to this dust, we find ourselves facing one of those astonishing, inexplicable facts which, like the Transverberation itself, may at some future day be declared a miracle by the Court of Rome. Our end is to discover, not the cause, but the meaning of the mystery, and we believe it may be found in an attentive consideration of St. Teresa herself.

On the last pages of this book, the reader will find a panegyric we pronounced upon her in 1875, the same year Father Cardellach published his pamphlet. It was an exposition of the fundamental aspect under which St. Teresa should be considered, an aspect containing the key to this treasury of wonders God has enclosed within her. The reader will there see proven that this illustrious woman was, by excellence, the Spouse of Christ, who was pleased to unite in her an exceeding great number of the qualities distinguishing the Spouse of the Sacred Canticles. There could be, and there have been in the opinion of some, virgins purer, more filled with love of God, more holy than Teresa; but none perhaps presenting, in so high a degree, the wonderful qualities of the mystical Spouse. We hope the reader will reflect upon this panegyric, and be convinced of the truth of our words.

Ah! it is a happy thought that reveals to us the mystical meaning of the dust, found at the bottom of the crystal containing the venerated heart of Avila's virgin. In Chapter III, verse vi, of the Canticle of Canticles, we read these words: *Quæ est ista, quæ ascendit per desertum, sicut virgula fumi ex aromatibus myrrhæ, et thuris, et universi pulveris pigmentarii?* "Who is she that goeth up by the desert, as a pillar of smoke of aromatical spices of myrrh and frankincense, and of all the powders of the perfumer?" Hence, we say to those who consider this dust natural, well, suppose it be so? The admission just now appears to us of slight moment, for we are striving to see if the allegorical words of Solomon's epithalamium were not fully verified in Teresa, both during her life and in her blessed heart after death. That pillar of smoke, is it not these abundant exhalations for so many years arising from this blessed heart, *sicut virgula fumi*;—the desert across which the Spouse travels—may it not likewise be found in the aridity and barrenness of this organ;—the perfumed powders, the aroma of myrrh, the grains of incense, are they not all represented by this dust of different species, and these dark grains encrusted upon her heart?

This same mystical picture was before us, when in Chapter VII, speaking of the great black spots, we quoted these words of the Spouse: "I am black, but beautiful. Do not consider me that I am brown because the sun hath altered my color."

That the marvels of our holy Mother's heart we have already recounted, and those we are going to mention, may have an eloquent allegorical signification, is sustained by her own revelations to a religious, an incident to which we have alluded. She told this religious, that the little stones around the heart represented the virtues adorning it. Why should not the other wonders be equally significant, especially when the allegorical images designating the Spouse of the Canticles, and the Valiant Woman of the Book of Wisdom, are all applicable to her? These phenomena, even divested of any miraculous character, and considered merely as marvels inexplicable to human understanding, praise God no less than all other natural wonders of this world.

A similar explanation may be given of the most beautiful of these phenomena—the appearance of thorns around the heart of the Seraph of Carmel. Did not the Divine Lover say to the object of His love: "As a lily among thorns, so is my beloved among the other daughters of Israel?" Could there be a more beautiful panegyric upon St. Teresa?

Father Cardellach seems never to have thought of this explanation, for on page 71 of his book, he recounts other particulars, the Biblical sense of which is clearly indicated. "Besides the dust," says he, "we find grouped on the anterior side of the heart, at the left of its lower extremity, certain heaps of whitish threads, like clippings of a woolen cord. Also, at the lower extremity of the posterior side, where the two brass wires suspending the heart cross, are seen other threads resembling scraps of yellowish wool. These seem as if *placed there expressly*, whilst the whitish ones appear to have fallen by chance. We can give no explanation of them save conjectures, just as we have in regard to the dust."

The excellent Missionary is so struck with the picture presented to his mind, just as he has described it above, the tufts of wool *placed there expressly*, and the clippings of cord apparently fallen by accident, that he confesses his ignorance, adding even that reason is a blind guide as regards the sense of this mystery. But without going so far, we find a satisfactory explanation in reflecting upon what the Holy Spirit tells us in the Book of Proverbs about the Spouse: "Who shall find a Valiant Woman? the price of her is as of things brought from afar off, and from the uttermost coasts. The heart of her husband trusteth in her, and he shall have no need of spoils. She will render him good and not evil, all the days of her life. She hath sought wool and flax, and hath wrought by the counsel of her hands." Behold the wool and linen woven by the Spouse's hands. The former is represented by the yellowish tufts like shreds of wool, the latter by the whitish threads so clearly and artlessly described by Father Cardellach. He designates them as clippings of cords or cinctures, and lo, the Holy Book says that the Spouse sells her handiwork to the merchants of Chanaan: "She made fine linen and sold it, and delivered a girdle to the Chanaanite."

In another place the author speaks of a substance resembling half ground rice, found at the lower extremity of the heart; and does not this also recall the Valiant Woman who gives food to her household? *Deditque praedam domesticis suis, et cibaria ancillis suis.* Does it seem likely that chance alone could have been the author of these striking analogies Let our readers judge for themselves.

XII.

Roots, Little Branches, and Other Peculiar Objects in St. Teresa's Heart.

Over much of the surface of this holy relic, we see distinctly excrescences resembling ivy roots, quite short, not more than one-seventh of an inch in length, and with corresponding ramifications. "They all take a horizontal direction, with a slight tendency upward or downward," says Father Cardellach. Our attention is attracted particularly by those springing directly from the heart, very near its lower extremity, and on the right of the spectator when facing the wound. One of them arises from this point in irregular undulations, almost parallel with that portion of the second organ. It is less than four-fifths of an inch long, and has divers radicles which give it the appearance of a little branch or a sprig of olive. It is as thick as a fine needle, and its color very clear cinnamon.

Another root is seen in the posterior view; arising from the side towards the point of the heart, and perhaps less than one-twenty-fifth of an inch from the bottom of the vase; it ascends about four-fifths of an inch, touching the glass at irregular intervals. It also has little branches, with drooping leaves, but it has no point. Its color at the root is whitish, gradually approaching a cinnamon towards the extremity. It is not visible from the front of the heart.

"These objects," says Father Cardellach, "that I call roots or branches, give to the Saint's heart an aspect *inexplicably arboriform*. I find no natural explanation of any of these phenomena, and science so far has been baffled. Still less could I explain the new prodigy of the thorns." He then gives mystical and figurative explanations, worthy of his lively faith and piety, which are apparent on every page. We cheerfully concede to all these explanations their proper value, but, nevertheless, returning to our fundamental idea that God was pleased to unite in St. Teresa the plenitude of gifts of the Spouse in the Canticles, we beg our readers to consider the image of the *enclosed garden.*

Let us indeed open Solomon's wondrous "Canticle of Canticles," and we shall find in chapter IV, these words of the Lover: "My sister, my spouse is a garden inclosed, a garden inclosed, a fountain sealed up," and a little below this we read: "The fountain of gardens; the well of living waters, which run with a strong stream from Libanus. Arise, O north wind, and come, O south wind, blow through my garden, and let the aromatical spices thereof flow." In chapter V, we again find this allegorical garden; it is the

Spouse who speaks, saying: "Let my Beloved come into his garden and eat the fruit of his apple trees," and the Lover answers: "I am come into my garden, O my sister, my Spouse." This image of the garden recurs in chapter VI, when the Spouse exclaims: "My Beloved is gone down into his garden, to the bed of aromatical spices, to feed in the gardens, and to gather lilies." A little below, on the same page, the Lover says: "I went down into the garden of nuts to see the fruits of the valleys." And finally, in chapter VIII and last of the Sacred Canticles, the Lover says to his blessed Companion: "O thou that dwellest in the gardens, the friends hearken: make me hear thy voice."

These wonderful Scriptural allegories, in my opinion, explain the mystery of the roots, the little branches, the stems and shrubs surrounding St. Teresa's heart. It is fortunate Father Cardellach did not perceive the analogy, for then the *inexplicably arboriform* aspect that he so ingenuously acknowledges struck his eye, would have appeared far-fetched, and the result of a preconceived idea. What thinks the reader? And again, is not the ivy clinging to the tree, so vividly represented by the sacred organ, figurative of that spiritual vine of the mystical Spouse forever united to the Lover, with whom she forms but one being?

The pious Missionary also notes a sort of trunk, more resembling a little stick than a thorn, and twisted after the manner of certain isolated shoots that spring from the principal trunk, and serve no other purpose than to prove the health and luxuriance of the plant. It extends horizontally, and meets the great pointless thorn. In the first lithograph it is marked number 17. These trunks, or stems, have also their signification. The Spouse of the Canticles complains of having been struck by the guardians of the city. *Invenerunt me custodes qui circumeunt civitatem: percusserunt me et vulneraverunt me.* "The keepers that go about the city found me: they struck me and wounded me." How truly were these words verified in St. Teresa, who had so much to suffer, and in so many ways, even from persons whose intentions were good in the sight of God!

Another object, still more curious and extraordinary, is seen in the long, bright flat thread which, springing up to the left of the spectator, and in the anterior portion of the heart, passes to the other side, and rises far above the pointed thorn. It is slender and shining like a pin; its color that of a dark platinum. Its course upwards, is very irregular, and almost in the centre is a knot, such as we often see in a twisted branch whose development is retarded. Beside it, between this thread and the heart, arises another point of the same nature. The nuns say these threads were not visible at first, when the other phenomena attracted their attention, at least they did not perceive them. They moreover affirm that they have grown perceptibly since their appearance.

On the 18th of May, 1875, Tuesday of Pentecost week, at half-past four in the afternoon, Father Cardellach noticed, for the first time, near a group of five exceedingly fine thorns, a little point darker than these threads. When one was directly facing the reliquary it escaped observation, but by stooping and looking up it was very perceptible. Its length was about one twelfth of an inch, perhaps a little less; it is nearer the centre than the other thorns discovered the same day, being about twice the distance from it that they are from one another. These all spring from the dust back of the heart, and it is easy to see that they have a common origin. This point is designated as number 25 in the second lithograph.

After all we have said it is not difficult to discover the sense of these threads. The Valiant Woman of the Scriptures, is represented as knowing how to manage the spindle and distaff. *Digiti ejus apprehenderunt fusum:* "Her fingers have taken hold of the spindle." Do we

not see in these words, the mystical meaning of
the long knotted threads among the other
wonders of St. Teresa's heart? And the rapid
growth of these threads, is it not significant of the
works of Christ's true Spouse? From this point
of view especially, do the hitherto inexplicable
marvels, specified and described by the Spanish
author with so much simplicity, and the candid
acknowledgment that he did not comprehend
their meaning, become more truly *wonderful*, if
we may be permitted to use the expression.
What eloquence in these mute signs! What
mysteries in these enigmatical emblems springing
forth one knows not how! What rays of light
escaping from this humble crystal, guarded so
carefully at Alba de Tormes!

XIII.

The First Five Thorns of St. Teresa's Heart.

Among all the wonders of St. Teresa's heart,
these are more especially the subject of the present work.

We call thorns, certain thorn-shaped excrescences or spontaneous productions, seen in the
crystal receptacle containing this blessed heart.
They appear to spring from the dust at the bot-

tom of it. There was no mention of them in the process of 1725, drawn up for the Transverberation, though allusion was made to a light vapor or smoke obscuring the inner sides of the crystal. Hence, we may reasonably infer that they must have appeared since, as it is not likely that anything so remarkable could have escaped observation.

The political tempest of 1836 swept over Spain; impiety stalked triumphant; thousands of religious were driven from their convents and forced, like scattered doves, to seek, wherever they could, a solitary branch upon which to rest their weary feet. How many vines were thus ruthlessly laid low in their best years! How many temples of the Lord were destroyed by the blasts of this revolutionary storm! What blood and what tears flowed!

The terrible tempest was over; after reciting Matins, the eve of March 19, Sister Paula of Jesus, at first Vespers of St. Joseph, making a visit to St. Teresa's heart, was greatly astonished to perceive the first two thorns! When discovered they were very small, much shorter and more slender than at present. By June, 1870, they had grown to a length of more than two inches. This gradual, though slow growth, would seem to indicate that their development was subsequent to the year 1835.

On the 27th of August, 1864, the day these religious, together with the whole Carmelite family, celebrated the Feast of the Transverberation, a third thorn was discovered. It was then very tiny, like the point of a pin, but in 1875 it would have measured an inch in length.

The good Carmelite Mothers thought they saw a fourth, but could not say positively. Doctors Elena, Sanchez, and others of their profession, verified the fact of its existence. It was then scarcely one-sixth of an inch long.

In 1875, May 3, Feast of the Finding of the Holy Cross, Father Cardellach visited the Saint's heart a second time. Placing the reliquary upon the window-sill, and regarding it attentively, he not only distinctly perceived the fourth thorn, but likewise a fifth, springing up near the root, at the base of the great pointed thorn. It is one thorn engendered by another, and is about as thick as the third discovered in 1864. The point whence it issues is towards the left of the heart, and the right side of the spectator, looking at the posterior portion of this organ. It is a sort of hook, of horizontal growth, extending along the surface of the dust, which nearly covers it, and seems to conceal the point. Its length is at least one-seventh of an inch. For this discovery, and all subsequent ones, he used the sunlight concentrated by means of a lens.

To assure himself of the fact, he asked the Mother Prioress and two other religious who were present, to examine carefully by the glass the lower extremity of the heart, especially the spot whence the great pointed thorn seems to spring. They did so, and the existence of the fifth thorn was placed beyond a doubt. This discovery somewhat excited Father Cardellach's curiosity, and on taking leave, he told the religious that, with their permission, he would visit them very soon again.

He returned on the 7th of the same month. Taking the reliquary into an upper room, so as to have more light, he again, by means of a lens, concentrated the sun's rays upon the lower extremity of the heart. His opinions as to whence these thorns spring were confirmed. Descending from the end of the heart, just between it and the brass wires holding it suspended, appeared a thorn. However, of this he could not assure himself, although he spent some time in examining with the lens the dust lying in the bottom of the receptacle. He now turned his attention to the two great thorns, and made the following observations: 1st. They are firm, slender, shining, smooth and pleasing to the eye—their color is a cinnamon; 2d. They are not round, but angular lengthwise, like a nail. He does not remember whether this angular form disappears at the pointed extremity.

He also remarked that the third thorn is without point, not that it has been broken, but because it terminates in a tuft, as it were, of very fine plumes, each like a dart. We should bear in mind, that this thorn appeared on the very Feast of the Transverberation. Those who discovered it, thought at first that it might be nothing more than a dilated pellicle.

Such is the history of the discovery of the first five thorns (1836—1875).

XIV.

Discovery of Five More Thorns.—The Knocks Heard in the Saint's Sepulchre.

That same day, May 7, 1877, Father Cardellach shifted the position of the crystal vase, so as to examine it from every possible point of view. Placing it between the limpid azure of heaven and his eyes, and looking at it sidewise, as far as the construction of the reliquary would permit, he most unexpectedly distinguished five more thorns. Filled with emotion, he rendered thanks to God. But to place their existence beyond doubt, he called the Mother Prioress, and asked her to look, designating the spot upon which she should fix her eyes. With great joy she perceived the five new thorns, and two other Sisters experienced the same satisfaction. Still Father Cardellach hesitated; they might be only rays of the crystal; the fineness of the lines was such that it left great room for doubt. He now changed the position of the reliquary, and was soon assured that he had made no mistake; the five new thorns were certainly there. He lifted up his heart anew in thanksgiving to Him who wrought such wonders. This visit was on a Wednesday.

On Thursday, May 13, the good Missionary repaired a fourth time to the convent. On this occasion he made no discoveries, but, renewing his former investigations, he was more fully convinced of the correctness of his conclusions. Everything he took note of with scrupulous fidelity, not even omitting to mention a singular incident that forcibly impressed him.

Seated near the window in the upper chamber, examining the thorns and trying, if possible, to discover whence they issued, he was startled by a noise from the crystal as if it had been struck by a grain of sand or the head of a pin. He turned it, and looked most carefully to see what accident had befallen the glass. "Was it the little tap that troubled you?" asked a religious.

"Yes, sister," he replied; "I was afraid the glass was broken." "Oh! that is nothing," said the Carmelite. "These blows or knocks are sometimes repeated so often during our prayers, that they are almost a source of distraction. Those from the Saint's sepulchre have been heard by the Community, and on one occasion we counted a number exactly equaling that of the men, who came into the chamber to take an inventory of its contents."

The missionary now inquired into the nature of these noises heard in the Saint's sepulchre, and after mentioning some well-authenticated facts regarding them, he gives us an idea of his opinion on the subject. We quote his words:

"A few days before the revolution of September, 1868, there were heard in the choir noises like the shivering of the picture glasses, on one occasion especially, when two or three nuns who were there, ran immediately to see if the glasses were not broken; but they found nothing disturbed. At other times, the windows of the choir emitted sounds like those that struck my ear in the chamber above. An aged religious of seventy years, simple as a child and very edifying to the whole community, heard during their religious exercises, though no one else did, a great noise in the choir, as of men walking through, their heels striking the floor. 'What is that! who are passing through?' she exclaimed. 'No one,' replied the other religious. And so it was. They saw and heard nothing.

"Some time after the revolution the Mother Prioress, at eleven o'clock at night, after reciting Matins, was in the room above the tomb. Deeply troubled lest they should all be driven from their convent, she was revolving these sad thoughts in her mind, when suddenly quite a loud knock was heard from the Saint's tomb. At first she deemed it an illusion, but when a second and a third followed she was terrified, and hastily descending, ran to the cell of the Sister who wrote the account. The latter had that instant entered. Seeing the Prioress in tears and evidently much affected, she inquired the cause. 'O, Sister! they are going to drive us from our convent. I have just heard three loud knocks from the Saint's sepulchre.' Though very timid and fearful herself, the other religious, to reassure her, answered: 'Oh! no, Mother. The Saint rather wishes by that to banish our fears, by reminding us that she is here to aid us.'

"Two other religious, another day, the date of which the person who related it had forgotten, heard in the Saint's tomb seven more knocks. Of course they were greatly alarmed. Some time later, when the enclosure of the monastery was violated, for the purpose of getting an inventory of its contents, it was noticed that the number of men was just ten, exactly the number of knocks that had been heard from the Saint's tomb—first three and then seven."

Father Cardellach also mentions, that once a noise was heard in the sepulchre like that of a body turning over. He himself had heard five light blows some days previously, but had not paid much attention to them. Were they not indicative of the five new thorns, just discovered? Or rather, the hour being one of silence and prayer, might not the Saint have wished to remind those present of recollection and more exact observance of the rule? Such were Father Cardellach's observations to the religious, but they assured him that under other circumstances they had likewise heard knocks, the meaning of which they could not comprehend. As for us, we believe that an attentive consideration of the Book of Canticles we have so often quoted, will give the key to these mysterious knocks. Are they not prefigured by these words of the Spouse: "The voice of My Beloved knocking: Open to Me, My sister, My love?" *Vox dilecti mei pulsantis: Aperi, soror mea, amica mea.* From this point of view, these phenomena seem to be in harmony with all the others relating to this blessed heart.

The Missionary asserts, that by turning and

re-turning the reliquary, he was fully convinced of the existence of the five new thorns, for if the very fine objects he saw had been only rays of the glass and not thorns springing from the dust, they would have been obscured by the latter in some of the various shiftings of the reliquary. On the contrary, these lines always appeared the same—smooth, whitish and shining, independent of one another, some near the glass, others a little behind these, crossing or separating, according to the point whence they were observed.

Every one can imagine the joy caused by such a discovery.

XV.

New Thorns Discovered May 18, 1875.

On the 18th of May, Father Cardellach repaired to the convent, according to his expression, to bid the Saint good-bye, as he was going to Cantalapiedra to give a mission. Entering this holy place for the last time, he kissed, as usual, the floor of the cell (now transformed into an oratory by the religious), where the holy Mother Teresa had lived and died. He then ascended to the little chamber, and again made an examination of the heart. Already familiar with all the marvels of this blessed relic, he wished by this last investigation to confirm, beyond the shadow of a doubt, the reality of his former discoveries. He was eminently successful, and it filled his heart with veneration and love, which arose in praises to the holy name of God.

With the glass, he was directing the sun's rays sometimes upon one spot, sometimes another, when suddenly a few whitish, shining lines caught his eye. A cry of joy escaped him. "What is it?" eagerly inquired the religious. "See, see, here, here, look very carefully and steadily," said he. They did so, and like Father Cardellach, saw clearly another group of *five new thorns!* They are at the posterior of the heart, and, as usual, seem to spring from the dust. All the lower extremity of this sacred organ is surrounded by a forest of thorns, as it were. "What mystery indeed can all these thorns signify?" exclaimed the worthy Missionary.

He perceived also, at the base of the long-pointed thorn, something like a black segment or part of a circle, that he supposed at first a shadow produced by the thickness of the glass in that place. It could easily be something else, said he, but I am not sure of it, nor have I any serious probability on the subject. So much that was new and wonderful, astonished him and filled his heart with satisfaction. That very day he heard five little knocks from the crystal reliquary, exactly the number of thorns he had just discovered.

As he was leaving the room, having pressed his heart to the reliquary, a sixth knock was heard in the crystal. "The Saint is very polite," said one of the religious, "she bids your Reverence good-bye." Father Cardellach, kissing the sacred relic, respectfully restored it to its place in the turn, and then taking leave of the Saint and her blessed daughters, he went away, his heart filled with holy remembrances. "This sanctuary," said he, "has stolen my soul. Could I but fix here my last resting-place!"

And it was thus, the devoted servant of St. Teresa had the happiness of discovering eleven thorns, including that which springs from the great pointed thorn in the form of a hook. He endeavors to connect the appearance of these thorns with the Revolution of 1868, which drove Isabella from Spain, and overwhelmed that unfortunate country with disasters. But as they were discovered several years after the Revolution, in our opinion, it seems rather far-fetched to attempt connecting the two events.

In conclusion, we will say, that without counting the excrescences, that Father Cardellach calls brass or iron wires, because of their resemblance to these objects; nor those he designates as roots or little branches, there have already appeared fifteen thorns, veritable thorns in shape and general outlines. The first two were discovered by the Carmelites, March 18, 1836; the third, likewise by the Carmelites, August 27, 1864. The fourth, we might say, was discovered by them, although the fact of its existence was confirmed only by the subsequent examination by the Doctors, of which we shall speak hereafter. All the rest, to the number of eleven, were first seen by Father Cardellach, a priest of the mission: the hooked thorn, May 3, 1875; five others, May 7; and, finally, five more on the 18th of the same month.

XVI.

Father Cardellach's Opinion as to the Origin of the Thorns—Their Signification.

It would never, for an instant, occur to any one looking at the two lithographs representing the opposite sides of St. Teresa's heart, that the famous thorns sprang from the lower extremity of the sacred organ. If these pictures are accurate, they certainly give the impression that the thorns, whose source or root still remains a mystery, partly concealed as they are by the dust at the bottom of the reliquary, do *not* spring from the sacred organ. Yet Father Cardellach frequently reverts to this his fixed, and we might say, favorite idea. We will not gainsay his opinion in the matter, both because he has been on the spot and most carefully examined the reliquary, and also, because in a short time, we may have positive proof that the lithographs, though designed with care, are incorrect.

On page 111 of his pamphlet, and several following pages, the author discusses this part of the subject. After expressing his individual opinion as to the *miraculous* nature of the thorns, he then gives his ideas concerning their origin, the point whence they spring. These considerations appear worthy of very great attention.

The religious affirm that in 1836, the epoch of the appearance of the first two thorns, the respiratory holes of the crystal heart were already closed with wax, and over this was a little linen cloth, still there in 1875. When these thorns were perceived, there was no dust at the bottom of the vase, merely a light vapor on the inside of the glass, as if it were tarnished. They positively assert that all the residuum at the bottom of the vase, or adhering to its sides, has made its appearance since the discovery of the thorns. Consequently, the dust can have no influence whatever upon their origin or preservation. This argument of Father Cardellach is not only weighty but decisive. The religious also declare that the thorns grew thicker as well as longer, though without any proportion between the two species of growth, one taking place later than the other.

Hence, continues the author, it is not possible that the thorns, at least the first ones, could have been developed from this dust, and much more impossible is it that the exterior dust could have had any part in their production from a vegetable germ, since the respiratory holes being closed, it could not penetrate the vase. And even supposing it could, the quantity must have been so infinitely small, as to have been utterly without influence upon the development of any germ whatever.

But whence then do these thorns arise? At present, there is a very considerable residuum at the bottom of the crystal; whether it be composed of detached particles of the surface of the heart, like the crumbling ruins of an old edifice; the effluvia or gases arising from the holy organ; or rather launched forth from its lower extremity, like lava from an open crater, we know not; but certain it is, a sediment of this nature exists, no matter what its cause, and it hinders our seeing clearly and examining this end of the heart. We are forced to conclude from the above that the two lithographs before us are inaccurate, since they permit us to see the brass wires which cross under the heart and hold it suspended. The wires would not be visible here, were this portion of the heart covered by the dust, as has been stated.

To prove that the thorns are rooted in the left side of the end of the heart, Father Cardellach remarks that they all start from this point, but they cross and take different directions, acquiring color and strength according to their development. The thorns of the posterior side likewise arise from the same place. Hence, he concludes that the left side of the lower extremity of the heart (it would be on the right hand of the spectator viewing the lithograph), is the source, the root, the seed of these thorns. We must repeat, that the two pictures here given do not permit us to draw such a conclusion.

Can the thorns, he continues, spring from the dust, entirely independent of the heart just opposite? Can they subsist without adhering to it? Can they find sufficient root and aliment in the dust? No, it is not possible for them to spring to life, to grow and retain life without other foundation than this in dust. And why not? Because the dust itself is even dryer, more arid than

the heart, which physicians, upon examination,
have declared dry, arid, mummified, absolutely
unproductive. Again, the dust is not cohesive,
it does not form a compact mass, capable of
affording steady support to any excrescences,
much less productions of the nature we are now
considering. These reflections, it is true, though
demonstrating that the thorns have not their
origin in the dust, are equally weighty against
the supposition of their springing from the heart
itself.

The following argument, however, appears to
us conclusive in favor of the latter opinion.
The thorns are not perpendicular, but more or
less inclined; not one but in rising forms an angle
of twenty-six or twenty-eight degrees. They
appear to spring up from the crystal itself, and
even without the support of the dust; hence, it
would be absolutely impossible for them to maintain their erect position, much less one inclined,
were they rooted in this variable, unstable foundation. The reliquary has indeed been moved
about a great deal, and has sustained many
knocks, both involuntary and intentional. If
the thorns were born of this dry, arid, inorganic
dust, with no cohesion between its molecules,
how is it they are not twisted, broken, or fallen
in the numerous shiftings and shocks to which
the reliquary has been subjected ?

On the contrary, admitting that they spring from the heart, their steadiness of position is, in a measure, explained. Father Cardellach again mentions in this connection, his slight blows upon the glass. He says that before the discovery of the last two groups of thorns, when he as yet knew of the existence of but four thorns, he attempted to ascertain if they sprang from the heart. For about five minutes, he struck with the ends of his fingers against the side of the crystal where there was least dust, hoping thus to scatter the groups, or produce an equilibrium that might allow him to see clearly beneath the point of the heart. But the result was far from satisfactory, though he did succeed in obtaining a partial equilibrium, some particles detaching themselves from the one side of the crystal, and forming themselves into groups on the other. This inorganic mass, as is usual in such cases, seemed to sway and then settle itself, but it apparently did not affect either the thorns or the roots. At these hits on the reliquary the heart moved, the excrescences also a little, the dust changed place, but no accident whatever happened; the thorns were in nowise affected. The religious really dreaded the breaking of some of them, but the Missionary himself had not the shadow of such a fear.

From this experiment he was convinced more

firmly than ever of the truth of his favorite idea, that the thorns derive their support from the heart itself, in which they are rooted. On the 7th of May, his third visit, he discovered five thorns. They were very fine, like the tiny bones of little fishes. They were of different sizes, as regards length, and not one of them broke under the blows he gave the crystal. At his last visit, on the 18th of May, he discovered, after a long time, five more thorns, two of them very long and so fine as to be almost imperceptible; to distinguish them it was necessary to fix the eye steadily upon the spot. But how is it that these, no more than the larger, were disturbed by the blows upon the reliquary? How could they remain motionless, firm, unbroken amidst this mass of moving dust? May we not infer hence, that they have a solid foundation, and where can this be found if not in the heart itself?

The author now asks, what is the nature or material of these thorns? He confesses his ignorance, but adds that the largest seem to be a vegetable production; the smallest, more on the animal order, something like a hair, though doubtless both belong to the vegetable kingdom. The former, he says, resemble the very long thorns of certain species of briars, but their color is decidedly that of cinnamon. The latter might be taken for bristles, or the tiny bones of microscopic fishes, yet they, likewise, are cinnamon colored at the extremity. Hence, he concludes their identity of species, which opinion is confirmed by the fact of their common origin.

Notwithstanding our desire to endorse Father Cardellach's belief, that the thorns spring directly from St. Teresa's heart, we are forced to maintain that the two lithographs of the heart do not give that impression, though, no doubt, our opinions would be in full accord with his, had we been on the spot and enjoyed the privilege and happiness of examining the reliquary as he did. These pictures, designed we believe under his direction, represent the heart suspended in an erect or perpendicular position, and the thorns all more or less inclined. How then could the thorns issuing from this sacred organ, form an angle far below the point of the heart?

He answers this difficulty, by supposing that they descend perpendicularly from the bottom of the heart until, coming in contact with the glass, their downward growth is checked; they then make a turn and ascend through the dust, appearing on its surface at different points and with different degrees of inclination. We candidly confess, that we cannot fully admit this opinion upon mere conjecture; some proof is needed to convince us. This downward growth of thorns, their curvature and upward growth, produced by an obstacle more likely to break them or arrest their progress, are certainly very singular. We must also note here, that since 1870, the religious are likewise of the opinion, that the thorns issue immediately from the heart, as we shall perceive from a document they have furnished. We, too, incline to this opinion, though not thoroughly convinced of it.

As to the mystical meaning of this marvel, the principal of those God has more recently wrought in St. Teresa's heart, we believe it may readily be found by recalling the text of the Canticles we have placed at the head of this little work. Among the eulogiums of the celestial Lover to His Spouse, is the following: "As the lily among thorns, so is my love among the daughters." *Sicut lilium inter spinas, sic amica mea inter filias.* Mgr. Martini, commenting upon these words and applying them to the Church, remarks: "Not only does the Spouse call His Church a lily, but in comparing her to human societies living upon earth, yet separated from her, the Jews, Gentiles, heretics, etc., he says, that she differs from them as absolutely as the lily from thorns, surpassing them in as great a degree as the lily excels the thorn." And thus God, apparently wishing to exalt St. Teresa above all the virgins of her day, as the grandest, most beautiful, most noble and famous, makes her heart appear triumphant in the midst of thorns; signifying by this her superiority over the rest of her sex, who, in comparison to her, are as dry and arid as these thorns.

Again, the thorn is symbolic of suffering and affliction; and no one will deny that St. Teresa had her share of these—her cup was filled to overflowing. And hence we may reasonably consider these fifteen thorns, as the sensible image of her heart's daily martyrdom, ending only with life. Though tasting spiritual sweetness, she likewise experienced all the sufferings of the Spouse in the Canticles, and perhaps our knowledge of what she endured, is slight in comparison to the reality. We may then say, in conclusion, that the recent wonders of St. Teresa's heart, as well as those of an earlier date, may be considered a palpable eulogium of God Himself upon this incomparable virgin.

THIRD PART.

The Recent Wonders of St. Teresa's Heart,
as Viewed by the Light of Science.

I.

An Official Report of the Discalced Carmelites of Alba de Tormes.

Ere completing our work, we deem it advisable to reproduce, under a purely historical aspect, the divers and even conflicting sentiments of very reliable individuals, as to the real origin, natural or supernatural, of the thorns which, for nearly forty-five years, have been forming a crown, as it were, around the blessed heart of the holy Mother, St. Teresa. This historical narration will not and cannot contain, either implicitly or explicitly, what, in the sight of God, is our opinion on the subject, but it will nevertheless furnish the reader with sufficient foundation to form one for himself.

We begin by quoting a very important document, inserted by Father Cardellach in his work, on pages 77 and 78. The venerable religious, who, in 1870, composed the Community of Discalced Carmelites at Alba de Tormes, unanimously signed, on the 5th of June, the following official report, which they remitted to the Most Reverend Father General of the Order:

"There were then three thorns, and we thought we saw a fourth, just beginning to appear on the right side of the heart, but as to the latter we could not say positively, *and these thorns seem to come from the lower extremity of the holy heart, and to take an upward course.* The first two were discovered by a religious named Paula of Jesus, now dead. It was in the year 1836, on the eve of the feast of our holy Father St. Joseph, after matins, and in the middle of the night, she saw them for the first time, and next day, the Feast of the holy Patriarch, all the religious saw them, two of which witnesses are still living.

"These two thorns are one each side of the heart, and in 1836, when first seen, they were very small, but they have grown gradually, and are now two inches long. We are all witnesses of their present existence and size.

"We perceived the third, August 27, 1864, the Feast of the Transverberation of the Heart of our holy Mother Teresa of Jesus. This third was also very small, like the point of a needle. We have all seen its beginning and its growth, and we render testimony to the fact.

"Maria Teresa of Jesus, Prioress; Maria Candelas of St. Teresa, Sub-prioress; Maria Dolores of Jesus of Nazareth; Anne Raphael of the Heart of Mary; Maria Carmela of St. Augustine; Maria Teresa of Carmel; Maria Josepha of the Heart of Jesus; Andrea of St. John the Evangelist; Maria Emmanuella of the Blessed Sacrament; Maria Antoinette of St. John of the Cross; Prisca of Jesus; Maria Teresa of St. Thomas; Josepha Ignacia of the Heart of Jesus; Teresa Maria of the Holy Kings; Paula of the Saviour; Josepha Maria of the Blessed Sacrament; Antoinette of Jesus Maria."

We see appended to this document the names of twenty-seven religious in all.

When these good nuns remitted it into the hands of their Father General, he very prudently ordered them to bury it, as the saying is, or in other words, to let the matter rest, taking no action whatever in regard to it, either by word or deed. But God, says Father Cardellach (page 79 of his pamphlet), wishing to glorify His faithful spouse and servant, Teresa of Jesus, made the marvel so public, that to-day it is known all the world over. The Doctors and Professors of medicine and surgery, who examined, literally by the light of the sun, and figuratively by the light of science and reason, St. Teresa's blessed heart, have contributed greatly towards diffusing a knowledge of its marvels;

their opinions and conclusions on the subject, those unfavorable to the supernatural view of the case, no less than those of the contrary, proving the fact of their existence.

II.

The First Opinions, those of Doctors Elena Alfonso and Sanchez Lopez.

In the chronological order of events, the opinions of the two doctors of medicine and surgery, Don Emmanuel Elena Alfonso and Don Dominique Sanchez Lopez, should head the list, as it was they who, in July, 1872, and August, 1873, drew up the first formula, and framed the first judgment, upon these phenomena, an abridgment of which document we give below.

After examination, they write out a very detailed description of St. Teresa's heart. In their opinion, the dust at the bottom of the crystal vase, is composed of particles detached from the heart's outer covering. The thorns, four in number, two on the right, two on the left of the holy organ, have their origin in this dust. They then give the measure of these thorns, and observe that the point of one is blunted, in consequence of its rubbing against the sides of the glass. They represent the heart as withered and arid, adding, that they perceive nothing whatever in the Saint's arm like to the appearance of the heart, although the circumstances and physical surroundings of the two relics are identical. Finally, they conclude by saying that, in their opinion, science is utterly powerless to give any satisfactory explanation of the origin and growth of these thorns, and that they do not hesitate to qualify the fact as supernatural and miraculous.

Such, in substance, is the judgment of these gentlemen, members of the Medical Faculty, a judgment, says Father Cardellach, which by its simplicity, its frankness, and logical sequence does them honor. Yet there are some points, continues he, upon which we are not in full accord.

First. They assert that the dust is composed of detached particles of the tegument or covering of the heart. Secondly. That the thorns spring from this dust. In our chapter describing the dust, we have adduced many strong arguments combating this opinion. Thirdly. They speak of four thorns, two to the right and two to the left. This is incorrect. It is true, that only four thorns had then been seen, but they were not arranged in twos each side of the heart; all sprang from the same trunk, the same spot, the same root. Fourthly. They mention that one thorn is blunted by reason of its coming in contact with the side of the reliquary; this might be the case, and yet an obstacle which retarded the downward growth of these excrescences, had an entirely different effect, causing them to change their course and ascend. Fifthly. As to the color and inequalities, we refer the reader to the chapter relating to them. The color of the thorns is a clear, bright cinnamon, at least, so they appeared to us (Father Cardellach). Sixthly. The observation regarding the arm is very much to the point. Seventhly. The consequence as to the supernatural character of these phenomena is logical, whether the thorns spring from the dust, or are rooted in the heart. Eighthly. They recognize an aridity of the heart no less than of the dust, and to such a degree as would render both utterly incapable of producing anything whatever, which conclusion we accept.

Such is an epitome of Father Cardellach's review of their opinion, which, he says, does them credit, candor and uprightness being gifts of God, attracting other blessings to their faithful possessors when these have been properly used.

III.

Another Opinion—That of Doctor Estevan Laurent.

In questions of very great moment, it is not only advisable, but even necessary, to weigh both sides, as no opinion whatever, no matter how well founded, is exempt in itself from the taint of error or passion. Remembering this, and anxious to obtain as impartial a judgment as possible, the Bishop of the Diocese, to these first two witnesses added a third, Don Jose Estevan Laurent, Doctor, Professor, honorary member of the Medical Faculty at the University of Salamanca.

These three doctors met in the little oratory (once the Saint's cell), at the monastery of the Incarnation of Alba, in presence of the ecclesiastical authority, and each one framed his judgment separately. We have already cited those of Doctors Elena and Sanchez, and it now remains for us to acquaint our readers with that submitted by Doctor Estevan, in August, 1873. He also gives a description of the heart after carefully examining it with a glass; he fully endorses the statement of his companions as to its utter aridity and mummification, and says, that the sediment is composed of the crumbling superficies of the heart, and likewise of the dust which found its way into the vase during the many years the respiratory holes were open. The productions called thorns, he thinks, are independent of the heart, and originate from the dust. They have, he writes, *every appearance of a natural production, and there is nothing extraordinary or supernatural about them.* An error in such a matter, despite the author's good intentions, would supply the material for criticisms serving as a pretext for contemning and even denying true miracles. Indeed, the vegetable nature of these excrescences is beyond doubt, but we could not assign them to any especial vegetable order, unless they were taken from the glass and analyzed.

Such, in substance, is Dr. Estevan Laurent's opinion. Father Cardellach gives very especial attention to many points therein, and cites them, either by way of confuting or approving them fully and freely before God.

He first says, a false judgment upon any fact whatever, can have no influence even at a thousand leagues' distance, in casting discredit, much less denial, upon true miracles. If there are true miracles (and this is beyond doubt), would one deny them upon the sole pretext that some men had given a different name to a fact, whose marvelous character is as clear as day? We candidly confess that we cannot endorse Father Cardellach's observations on this point; for, as the Professor of Salamanca sagely remarks, a grave error detected in a fact, currently believed miraculous, would indeed prove a *pretext*, or in other words, furnish a foundation for foolish, precipitate judgment, discrediting and denying all miracles, true as well as false. This is so apparent, that the Church reserves to herself the exclusive right of decision in such cases, and precisely from motives identical with those the Professor so candidly expresses.

Every one knows that the exposure of a pretended miracle, or even the detection of a mistake in regard to a matter deemed miraculous, but in reality not so, could indeed weaken the faith of many in true miracles, and it is always well to guard against such dangers.

We continue Father Cardellach's arguments against the Professor's conclusions. The Doctor, says he, concludes that the origination of the thorns is natural and regular; in our opinion, this conclusion is not logical. And, indeed, from what he establishes as certain and evident, we deduce with certainty, that he cannot fix or determine the natural cause explaining this phenomenon. Decomposition cannot produce an organized being, regularly fashioned, several times repeated, and endowed with the power of reproduction. Decomposition, especially under the circumstances we are considering, absolutely brings forth nothing, for decomposition cannot form, nor destruction build, as is confirmed by the experience of all mankind.

When decomposition, corruption, or the destruction of any living thing whatever, produces some excrescence of apparently vegetable nature, it is never more than a species of mould or moss, more or less visible, which viewed through a microscope, somewhat resembles a plant, but is irregularly formed, lacking life, fecundity, or the power of conservation. This vegetation would also want the substances or juices absolutely necessary to any form of life, as is precisely the case of these thorns. The aridity observed in the examination of the heart, completely excludes all possibility of any natural vegetable production. Aridity and vegetation are diametrically opposed, and could not simultaneously exist, in the same body, the same spot, and surely not in a heap of dust. Aridity is conducive to dust, and dust presupposes absolute aridity. Vegetation, on the contrary, is suggestive of humidity, and humidity may produce vegetation. The thorns are regularly fashioned, stable, uniform, and endowed with the power of reproduction; they have now been in existence for forty years, are fresh and vigorous, and during this period, they have from time to time put forth new shoots. How can this be? Whence do they come? Acknowledge the prodigy! exclaims Father Cardellach, it will certainly be for you the best and most honorable, for in disavowing the miracle, you must admit a greater impossibility.

But, remarks the good Missionary, some will say, you do not know nature's secrets, and what occult forces she may have, capable of producing such excrescences. To this he replies: First: That nature is only a blind, mute servant of the Most High, acting ever in accordance with laws He has traced out. Secondly: That the works of nature are nothing more than the consequences of these laws imposed by God—that He sometimes suspends, suppresses, and varies them according to His good pleasure, which acts or derogations from the laws of nature are called miracles. Thirdly: That when man examines a fact, from a scientific point of view, he should never recur to occult forces for the explanation of what he does not understand. It would be entering a labyrinth, interminable, inextricable. You speak of occult forces, and yet they are mysteries to you. How then, can you discuss them, and attribute to them a power and efficiency superior to those of the ordinary laws of nature? Consequently, dismiss those from your mind, and consider only those with which you are acquainted. Do you really understand this phenomenon? If so, explain it. If not, confess your littleness, your blindness here, and recognize the hand of the Most High, the Author of wonders innumerable. It is undeniable that man does not fully comprehend nature, and that many of her laws are secrets to him; yet it is equally undeniable, that none of these hidden laws can be contrary to those that are known, for both are the work of the same author—God. Fourthly: Even admitting the existence of these hidden laws, we should never appeal to them, when the ordinary laws of nature should suffice for the formation of a judgment. We are called upon to examine not what is hidden, but what God has placed under our eyes, what is within our reach, embraced by the circle of human sciences, and governed by laws immutable. Fifthly: Nature of *herself* is powerless to produce or create; even when she receives from man's hand the seed and labor necessary to fructification, the benediction of God must be there, or human efforts fail, as we see every day. With how much greater hesitation should we venture to assert, that she has brought forth productions more extraordinary, beautiful, admirable, in all their surroundings, and the circumstances attending their appearance, more exuberant and fecund than could ever be expected from her ordinary laws, even under the most favorable auspices. Sixthly: The suggestion of extracting the Saint's blessed heart from the crystal vase, to carefully analyze it, and thus establish the truth, is not to be thought of for one instant.

And where seek the cause and explanation of this phenomena, were we to analyze the contents of the crystal receptacle—in the skin of the thorns, if they have one? in a crosswise or lengthwise examination of their fibres, if they have fibres? in the proportion of elements entering into their composition, in those minute, capillary tubes invisible to the naked eye, yet often found in such excrescences? Must we seek it in the strength of resistance they possess, in their savor or chemical properties, their connection with other productions to which they may have some resemblance? For my part, I believe that in none of these could the explanation of the prodigy be found; because no matter how scrupulous our examination of the pellicles, fibres, substance of the thorns or elements entering into their composition, our conclusions would always be confronted by this dry, mummified state of the heart, likewise of the sediment and dust, conditions diametrically opposed to vegetation. So, even the analysis would not enlighten us as to the truth, or make known to what species of the vegetable kingdom the thorns might belong. Such are Father Cardellach's arguments, page 84, of his pamphlet.

IV.

Another Opinion—That of Doctor Villar y Macias.

In the face of two such conflicting testimonies, or rather conclusions as to the origin of the thorns, it was at least advisable to have the opinion of a third party. Don Agen Villar y Macias, Doctor of Medicine and Pharmacy, Licentiate of the Sciences at the University of Salamanca, was called upon for this purpose. He immediately repaired to Alba de Tormes, visited the heart, examined it, and in January, 1872, framed his judgment upon the question.

He describes this heart, after a most careful examination with good lenses, and attests its state of utter aridity. He mentions the sediment found at the bottom of the crystal vase, and attributes it to detached particles from the heart, and perhaps ordinary dust also, which had penetrated the respiratory holes. The excrescences, in his opinion, have their origin in the dust. His conclusion is, that nothing definite can be decided upon the subject, without a thorough knowledge of the past history of the relic, and the precautions taken in transferring it to the different vases in which it was kept; for according to the religious, several of these were broken, in consequence, it was supposed, of the expansion of the gases escaping from it. Finally, he thinks that an analytical study is necessary, considering the difficulty of studying the holy organ enclosed as it is. In this manner, and taking into account all particulars connected with it, we might be able to reach some definite conclusion regarding the phenomenon, which is certainly *so remarkable from any point of view*, that the sciences may indeed be forced to declare themselves unable to explain it.

Our author (Father Cardellach) makes the following observations upon Doctor Villar's very indeterminate judgment. First: Don Villar demands a detailed history of the holy relic, including that of the several periods passed in the different vases, and all the precautions taken in transferring it from one to another. This information may be obtained from the verbal process drawn up at the beginning of the second quarter of the last century, when application was made to the Court of Rome, for the institution of an especial Feast in honor of the Transverberation of the heart of Teresa of Jesus. I believe, however, continues Father Cardellach, that this detailed account would be of very little value in assisting one to frame a judgment upon the thorns, which did not appear for more than a century later than the period here mentioned. Secondly : The fracture of former vases, be the cause what it may, has no more bearing upon the question as to whence the thorns spring, than has the preservation of the present reliquary, since neither circumstance could, in the slightest, affect the production of the prodigies. Thirdly : He attests the aridity of the heart, the independence of it, the thorns springing from the dust, the production of the sediment, and the number of thorns he has observed, all of which had been previously made known and commented upon. Fourthly: The author himself, in his opinion signed November 27, 1873, and written after his first and comparatively superficial examination of the heart in question and its phenomena, has already taken note of these various and minute particulars the Professor mentions; he has even observed more than the latter, and concludes that they can have no influence upon the productions remarked in the vase. Fifthly: Nothing definite would be likely to result from acting upon the Professor's suggestions, for indeed, after alluding to the necessity or expediency of analyzing a phenomenon, most remarkable from any point of view, he adds that the sciences may be forced to declare themselves unable to explain it satisfactorily. Sixthly: Considering the circumstances in which we find the heart and its adjuncts, even admitting Doctor Villar's judgment, we may truthfully say, without evasion or subterfuge, that the appearance of these thorns, and other excrescences already described, must ever remain an enigma for science.

Thus does Father Cardellach express himself in regard to Doctor Villar's report on the subject. Scrupulously adhering to our first function, that of compiler only, we give no opinion. Doubtless it would have been more satisfactory to his readers, had Father Cardellach reproduced in his pamphlet, the extire text of the judgments of these experts. No doctor, indeed, is answerable to the public for an abridgment of his ideas, strung together by another person.

V.

The Judgment Presented by Father Cardellach to the Bishop of Salamanca—Preliminary Observations—General Principles.

October 27, 1873, the Rev. Nemesius Cardellach presented to the Bishop of Salamanca, his written judgment upon the heart of St. Teresa. We give below, in substance, copious extracts from the corrected, modified account that he has inserted in his most conscientious work.

He begins by saying, page 87, that botany has no knowledge whatever of such a species of vegetation; that the circumstances under which these excrescences appeared, and in which they have maintained life and vigor, for more than forty years, is wholly abnormal. It is a mystery inexplicable to science, and this constrained silence of science, he interprets in favor of the prodigy. How our piety is augmented, and our soul elevated, by the consideration of these wondrous works!

He follows these premises by a series of eleven observations, in which, for the sake of clearness on the subject, he repeats much already known to our readers, from the previous portion of this book, and which consequently we omit here.

After these observations, he establishes general and theoretical principles, pages 89 and 90.

To weigh the matter carefully, says he, and corroborate by evidence of another nature, statements already made, I shall lay down a few principles, the application of which will prove an invaluable assistant in solving the difficulty. Founded upon these principles, admitted by all, our conclusion is beyond appeal.

First: Aridity of *itself* can never naturally

produce anything. Our daily experience proves that everything would perish without water.

Secondly: Natural vegetation is impossible without humidity. Farmers will give the reasons for this.

Thirdly: Like causes produce like effects under the same circumstances.

Fourthly: Air, in the present economy of Providence, is necessary to life, even in the vegetable kingdom.

Fifthly: An organized being supports life, by means of its connection with nutritive substances suitable to its nature and condition.

Sixthly: *Ex nihilo nihil fit.* From nothing is made nothing; which means that neither angels, nor man, nor nature, when the materials are wanting, can produce the least thing. To create belongs to God alone.

Seventhly: *Parum pro nihilo reputatur.* A little equals nothing; or in other words, one cannot sustain life or fashion an object with the minimum of the substance requisite; in a pinch of earth one could not plant a tree, or make it live; with a few grains of sand one could not build a house, or water a garden with a few drops of water, or live a long life with a breath of air; wherefore we say, a little equals nothing.

Eightly: What human science cannot satisfactorily explain, finds its natural explanation in God.

Ninthly: What is above or beyond the laws of nature, naturally falls under the direct dominion of the holy will of God.

Tenthly: When in any creature we can ascertain no cause of its origin, and that it lacks the necessary conditions of life, we must recognize a supernatural hand.

By the aid of these principles, says he, we shall discover the origin and root of the thorns; even as we have recognized it in divers points already treated, so will we in others yet to be considered. Adhere to these principles, and we shall surely be enlightened on the subject.

Love of truth however constrains us (the commentators) to add, that all these principles cannot be received in their full acceptation, because they are not all sufficiently precise and irrefutable to form the immutable basis of a miracle—for instance, the eighth principle. What human science cannot satisfactorily explain, finds its natural explanation in God. There is indeed an infinity of natural phenomena, many things of ordinary, daily occurrence, that human science, so far, has not been able to explain satisfactorily,—earthquakes, the nature of comets, the immediate cause of meteors, how clear, sweet, inexhaustible supplies of water remain in the bowels of the earth, and yet none of these are ever referred to the class of miracles. Where would such a principle lead us? If Father Cardellach intends to express by this, only the natural and ordinary intervention of God in regard to his creatures, we answer that such intervention is identically the same in events we can explain, and those escaping our explanations. Hence, though science declare its inability to account for the appearance and growth of these thorns, this fact is not sufficient to place the phenomena among miracles; we must take another step and apply the ninth principle, in other words, prove that this appearance and growth are beyond and above natural laws.

The author now follows this with five closely-written pages of reflections, which he says, are merely an amplification of these principles. We shall cite only his reply to the fifth objection, which was the possibility of the thorns having originated from certain seed that had accidentally found their way into the vase, through the holes of the lid. Such an objection it would be difficult to imagine, for how could seed penetrate to the inside of the receptacle when the holes were closed? However, let us listen to our author's replies.

Absolutely speaking, says he, since there were holes, the introduction of seed might be urged as the cause of these thorns and other excrescences, and yet such an introduction is, and can really be proved, an impossibility. Whence came these seeds ? How is it they are so far apart ? . . . Their results are always the same, a seeming thorn, without leaves, flowers, branches, visible roots or any of the ordinary accompaniments of vegetation ? How have they maintained life, developing both in size and numbers, for so many years, though deprived of everything necessary to the sustenance of vegetable productions of this nature ? How is that the two largest have not withered or died, since the long interval of their appearance, 1836 to 1873 ? What then is this plant ?

Did these seeds come from the country, and wafted by breezes across the city, did they enter the convent chapel, penetrate the turn, seek the reliquary, and finding the holes, introduce themselves into the receptacle, pass over the heart without stopping and descend to the dust, there to bury themselves ? And again, without juices or other aliment except that contained within themselves, they germinated, took root, and spontaneously sprang up in the shape of these vegetable excrescences !

And this most extraordinary production should bear a striking resemblance to a long, dry thorn ! . . . and there should be not one only, nor two, nor three, but fifteen ! Again, they are so far apart, and the phenomena so often repeated, yet it is always the same seed, the productions ever identical in shape and color, they arise from the visible portions of the heart, but always seeking the dust, bury themselves therein, afterwards to push their way through and ascend! . . . How does it happen that these seeds have not once even found their way into the reliquary containing the arm, which occupies the other half of the closet? From all which we draw the logical inference, that by no means, could any accident of this sort have produced these excrescences.

Father Cardellach's reasoning is very conclusive. The supposition that seed could have penetrated the crystal vase, is so much the more ridiculous, absurd, really beyond the province of discussion, inasmuch as, for a long time before the appearance of these thorns, the holes in the crystal vase had been completely closed.

VI.

The Spanish Author Concludes that the Origin of the Thorns is Miraculous.

We give entire the text of Father Cardellach's conclusion:

Having duly considered, after an attentive and careful examination, many times and by the help of good lenses, the mummified, dry, arid heart of St. Teresa of Jesus, hermetically sealed in a crystal vase protecting it from all direct atmospheric influence:

Having duly considered the sediment in the form of dry, arid dust, proceeding either from detached particles of the heart's envelopes, its condensed emanations, or crumbling fragments of the heart itself, which have fallen to the bottom of the vase:

Having duly considered the whole perfectly protected from the air, and equally so from humidity and heat, as far as the season and place permit:

Having duly considered the appearance in the interior of the vase, of fifteen vegetable excrescences in the form of dry thorns, (of different dimensions as they sprang forth at different periods, and some distance from one another), although the arid heart and dust are not of themselves, *ex se*, material calculated to bring forth any vegetable production:

Having duly considered the want of humidity, so indispensable to the germination of seed originating any vegetable production:

Having duly considered the privation (probable) of air indispensable to the generation and conservation of the plant:

Having duly considered that neither air, nor

seed, nor humidity, nor heat (probably) have, in this instance, concurred in a production fifteen times repeated, at different periods and different spots, and that consequently, the vase contained neither the substance nor the juices necessary to vegetation:

Having duly considered that the simultaneous existence of thorns or vegetable excrescences, appearing at various periods, should and must necessarily, according to natural laws, absorb for their existence and development aliment suitable to their nature and in proportion to their needs:

Having duly considered that this continued absorption must exhaust the enclosed juices, which may by chance have been at the bottom of the vase, and the excrescences ought, in consequence, to have been dry, withered and dead:

Having duly considered that so far from being in this state, according to the immutable laws of nature, the excrescences, on the contrary, have increased in numbers and size for the space of forty years, maintaining themselves in a great variety of dimensions, with all the vigor of their birth:

Having duly considered that it would have been impossible for man, even the wisest and most skilful, to have furnished the seed, likewise humidity, heat and air, in suitable proportions, for the formation and continued preservation of such vegetable productions as now occupy our attention:

Having duly considered the opinions of Doctors, as to the circumstances and condition in which this blessed heart is found; also, that science, so far, has been unable to give a satisfactory explanation of the appearance and continued existence of the fifteen thorns, roots and other phenomena remarked in the favored heart of the seraphic and mystic Mother, St. Teresa of Jesus, so carefully and religiously preserved in the exemplary Monastery of the Incarnation at Alba de Tormes:

In fine, having duly considered all the antecedents laid down in this little book, and reasoning upon the grounds here presented, leaving, however, to men of wisdom to discern their gravity and importance, and submitting unreservedly to the judgment and decisions of the holy Church, I believe:

First: That the excrescences called thorns, all germinate in and arise from the heart of St. Teresa of Jesus, preserved in a sealed crystal vase.

Secondly: That the thorns all spring from the lower extremity or point of the heart, the left of the wound made by the Seraph.

Thirdly: That each and every one of the objects contained in the vase is admirable; and that the thorns, considering all the circumstances of their appearance, development and preservation, surpass the laws of nature, are wonderful, miraculous, the especial work of God's own hand.

Such is my individual judgment upon the thorns, or excrescences, and other phenomena observed in the reliquary, enclosing the blessed heart of St. Teresa of Jesus at Alba de Tormes. I have endeavored, by these observations, to answer the opinions of doctors and the objections that have been presented, and without wishing to argue, I have sometimes given detailed explanations that might be regarded as superfluous.

I present these reflections in no official character whatever. They have been made with no scientific preparation, but merely as notes, wherein I express my great admiration of that human Seraph called Teresa of Jesus, and my infinitely higher idea of our Lord God Most High, who thus lets fall upon earth some sparks of His power, love and glory.

I adore God's designs in these wonderful manifestations of His ineffable goodness, and I most earnestly confess how great is the Lord in His saints, how magnificent and wise in all His works. May our Divine Redeemer be eternally praised and blessed.

NEMESIUS CARDELLACH.

SALAMANCA, November 27, 1873.

Such is the brief opinion or judgment of our excellent Spanish Missionary. All St. Teresa's children and clients should be truly grateful to him, for devoting so much time and attention, in bringing before the world this new glory of the Seraph of Carmel.

VII.

Gaps in our Spanish Author's Argument.

It cannot be denied, that there are some wide gaps in this wise judgment favoring the miraculous side of the question, which our author presents to the Bishop of Salamanca. His efforts, indeed, all tend to prove that the thorns cannot be of vegetable origin. We must admit that his arguments on this point are very strong, and it would be exceedingly difficult to answer these reflections, for they prove almost conclusively, the impossibility of any vegetable growth in the closed vase containing the Saint's heart. But the admission of all this, is still very far from establishing the miracle, because such a course of reasoning does not exclude the possibility of some other origin. The proofs of a miracle, must be such as preclude all possibility of any natural cause whatever. St. Anthony certainly worked a miracle when, moved by the excessive sorrow of a mother, he restored to her son the foot that had been cut off. The irrefutably miraculous character of this event, arises from the fact of there being no natural agent capable of producing such an effect. But Father Cardellach, in excluding one natural cause of the phenomena, has not thereby excluded all. And behold the source of perplexity. We say perplexity, for he suddenly found himself in a great perplexity, unable to reply, when a Spanish priest, whom he styles illustrious, observed that these thorns might be the result of an animal agent. Let us recount the circumstances.

August 5, 1875, he placed before a venerable priest, at Madrid, a *fac simile* of the holy Mother's heart. After examining it most carefully, and questioning Father Cardellach, who took great pleasure in imparting whatever information he possessed on the subject, this ecclesiastic suddenly propounded a question for which our Missionary was wholly unprepared. He observed, that there exists a species of polype whose life is spent in building their habitation —building it in such a manner, that they advance in their path as the construction of their house progresses. " I have seen," said this priest, " one of their works; it was about a foot long, and so slender and fine throughout, that it might have been taken for a horse hair. These polype are continually depositing new material, and thus advance as their work advances. Might there not be some agent of this kind in the case before us?" He held this language, with the sole view of putting his interlocutor in the way of answering any objection, that might one day be drawn from the existence of these polype.

The good Missionary was silent, not knowing what to say; for, indeed, he was very much struck with the strong probability of truth in this objection, and the consciousness of his having overlooked it, making a wide gap in the document he had remitted to the Bishop of Salamanca. At Valencia, August 18, 1875, he wrote to this objection a reply, and perhaps his longest, for it occupies seven very closely written pages. Little satisfied with it, the Madrid priest answered in these terms:

"As to my observations, they were meant more as an insinuation than an objection. I still adhere to what I have already said, that no doctor can pronounce upon this phenomenon, whether it be natural or supernatural, until he has most carefully and scrupulously examined it. I would suggest a microscopic examination, to see if it is not the work of some animal agent. The atmosphere of the crystal globe, this dust which seems to be a collection of particles of the same substance as the heart, make me suspect a living agency.

"I see no way of solving the difficulty (or doubt, as you are pleased to call it), I have raised, except by a minute, thorough investigation, for we cannot deny *a priori*, the possibility of this hypothesis. Should one assert that it is a gratuitous assumption, which may be denied without any proof, in my opinion this would be an error. Indeed, in a case of this sort, the proof must be given by him who affirms the existence of the miracle; he must show conclusively that the thorns, or objects which appear to be such, cannot be attributed to any agent, physical, chemical, vegetable or animal. As to any physical or vegetable agency in the present case, I think no one would assert it; but it is not thus in regard to a chemical agent, and still less so in reference to the supposition of the presence of animalcula.

"If the analytical examination cannot be made without exposing the holy relic itself, it would be better to let the matter rest, in hopes that God would, by some other means, manifest the signification of this most extraordinary fact. At all events, I believe it premature in itself, and dangerous for religion to affirm or deny what it is."

Such is, word for word, this illustrious priest's reply, says Father Cardellach. He (the latter) promises a complete refutation of it, point by point, as soon as he finds time to devote to the subject. And indeed, keeping his word, at least as to endeavors to refute, he begins an interminable and perplexing response, taken for the most part from the elements of zoology. It fills more than twenty-four closely printed pages, and the length of it alone will suffice to make one understand how difficult it is, in some cases, to prove a miracle. He devotes not less than fourteen pages, to establishing the impossibility of any animal agency.

The illustrious priest of Madrid was, it seems, not much better satisfied with this second answer, as appears from the following, written by him on the 27th of August, 1875, Feast of the Transverberation of St. Teresa's Heart.

"This matter of the thorns seems to me very intricate; however, it is evident, that if the work be God's own, He will furnish us with the means of dispelling all doubt or illusion. I beg your Lordship to be very slow in publishing anything but the facts themselves. The facts, to be sure, but to decide whether they are natural or supernatural is running too great a risk of disagreeable errors, and still worse consequences."

If the priest of Madrid was illy satisfied with

our author's replies, the latter was just as little pleased with those of the priest of Madrid. We refrain from citing Father Cardellach's lengthy arguments demonstrating the exclusion of any animal agent, and these are our reasons. First: The perusal of them would leave our readers in the same perplexity as before, if not greater, and those who had regarded the miracle undeniable, might begin to doubt it. Who indeed could put sufficient confidence in the author's knowledge of zoology, a study always more or less uncertain, as to found upon it the certitude of a miracle? Secondly: All animal agency being excluded, we are to begin again and go through another course of argument, because the proofs establishing this, do not exclude other natural agents, for example, fermentation or other chemical causes. In following this, our author's method of exclusion, we would not finish under a big volume. It had certainly been advisable for him to have pursued a shorter, clearer, more decisive method. Intricate, prolix demonstrations rarely serve their purpose. Thirdly: It is true we are not writing a book of piety, but it is a book intended especially for the devoted children of St. Teresa, and they surely would be wearied, were we to make them read the pages Father Cardellach has written upon polype, zoophites, marine plants, vermicules, flesh plants, etc. Fourthly:

We hope the few reflections in-the next chapter, will not only supply to our readers the place of the omitted arguments, but being shorter, will also prove more agreeable and decisive.

VIII.

The Existence of the Thorns is a Wondrous Work, Wherein We Trace the Especial Intervention of God's Hand.

Our readers have been made acquainted with the divers and conflicting sentiments of Spanish priests and laymen, as to the origin—natural or supernatural—of the famous thorns, and all Spain is filled with the noise of this phenomenon. Some have positively denied the miracle, others as positively affirmed it, whilst others have suspended their judgment. Two prudential motives, which we shall give as follows, bind us to absolute silence in regard to an opinion of their nature. First: The ecclesiastical authorities, both at Salamanca and Rome, hold the matter under investigation, and it is better to await their decision, which will have a double value, by reason of the supreme tribunal from which it emanates, and the rigid investigation preceding this decision. Secondly: Being at a distance from the place, it is impossible for us to assure ourselves on any doubtful point, in regard to which eye-witnesses may be in perplexity. Of course, were we merely relating our individual sentiments upon the subject, we would express ourselves more freely.

Leaving aside, then, the miraculous nature of the phenomenon, we will endeavor to establish, upon a solid foundation, what is really certain, and cannot be the object of discussion. This will furnish sufficient aliment for our own edification, and renewed rejoicing on the part of St. Teresa's servants, at the increased glory of their Mother.

The appearance of these thorns in 1836, their development and existence to the present day, together with the little branches, roots, dust, shreds of wool, the knotted threads, half-ground rice, is a fact certain and undeniable, never even mooted in the various judgments bearing upon it—a fact attested by thousands and thousands of eye-witnesses, and admitting not the shadow of a doubt. So much for our first premise.

Secondly: It is equally undeniable, that human science so far has been unable to give any satisfactory explanation of this phenomenon, the opinions even of those who oppose the idea of its supernatural origin, being uncertain and confused.

The heart of St. Teresa has become for the learned of this world a wondrous thing, baffling their knowledge, and causing them to draw their conclusions with *ifs* and *buts*, which consequently render these conclusions worthless.

Thirdly: It is certain that the fact is astonishing, interesting, wonderful, under any circumstances, and has excited the admiration of all who have seen or heard of it. The well-known proverb, "Astonishment is the Mother of ignorance," has been here exemplified, for science, so far, being declared incapable of explaining the phenomenon, has been forced to give place to astonishment and wonder.

Fourthly: It is certain that the phenomenon is new, it is unique, we find nothing like it, either in the natural or supernatural. Nowhere have we ever read anything similar. This of itself should set those to· thinking, who insist upon regarding it as purely natural, for as the Psalmist sings, the laws of nature are eternal. "He hath established them forever, and for ages of ages."[1] There exists no natural phenomenon, that may not be the repetition of what has already taken place somewhere or some time.

Fifthly: It is certain that the heart of St. Teresa, that favored abode of the Holy Spirit,

---

[1] Psalm CXLVIII.

that chosen sanctuary of Divine Love, that ardent furnace of charity, was during life and after death, the field of not marvels only, but true miracles wrought by God's hand, some of which have been attested by the Church, for instance, that of the Transverberation. And hence it is reasonable to believe, that veritable miracles may be followed by miracles, probable and apparent.

Sixthly: It is very certain that the thorns are not of vegetable origin, Father Cardellach's argument on this point being irrefutable. And it really seems equally difficult of belief, that God would have permitted worms, polype or other animalcula to form themselves within, or penetrate the crystal vase containing St. Teresa's blessed heart. God has a jealous care of the remains of His saints. Says the Psalmist: "The Lord keepeth all their bones: not one of them shall be broken." *Custodit Dominus, omnia ossa eorum: unum ex his non conteretur.*[1] The bodies of the saints can and do become the prey of worms, but we cannot believe that such would be the fate of a holy, miraculous relic, after its preservation for three hundred years.

Seventhly, and finally: it is certain, that the phenomena St. Teresa's heart has presented to

---

[1] Psalm XXXIII.

our consideration for the last forty-five years, even supposing them of the natural order, appear to be directed by an *Intelligence* that has ordered and arranged all for some mysterious purpose. And this is the thought completely escaping our Spanish author. He has spoken, it is true, of a mystical signification of the thorns, but he has never laid any stress upon the fact, that the principal agent in all these phenomena, even supposing them natural, is God. The dust, the thorns, the seeming shreds of wool, the rice, the little stones, the dart, the threads, the branches could never have been produced by a blind agent, such, for instance, as a chemical, vegetable, or animal agent. Evidently, throughout appear luminous traces of an Intelligence that, in our opinion, designs: First, to assimilate the heart of St. Teresa to that of Jesus, as we have already shown; secondly, to exemplify in the heart of St. Teresa all that distinguishes the Spouse in the Canticles, and this we have also shown. It is written of the Valiant Woman, the model Spouse, that "she seeks linen and wool," and lo! here are shreds of linen and wool; that "her fingers have taken hold of the distaff and spindle," and behold, the threads with their knots wonderfully formed; that "she hath given victuals to her maidens," and here is rice, the ordinary nourishment; that "she delivers a girdle to the Chanaanite," here are the clippings of cord. It is written of the Spouse of the Canticles that "as the lily amidst thorns, so is she in the midst of her companions," and behold Teresa's heart surrounded by thorns; that the Spouse "goeth up by the desert, amidst a pillar of smoke of aromatical spices of myrrh, of incense and all the powder of the perfumer," and behold Teresa's heart, visible amidst a heap of dust and objects resembling grains of incense and myrrh; that the Spouse was struck and wounded by the keepers of the city, and here we see the lance and rods, even symbolical of authority and chastisement.

But, say some, you at least insinuate the supernatural origin of these phenomena. We answer no, for the natural phenomena in which the directing intelligence of God appears are numberless; in proof of which assertion we need never have recourse to a miracle properly so called, that is, a suspension of the laws of nature. Look at a piece of honeycomb made by the bees, and do you not clearly perceive that a wise intelligence has surely presided over this admirable work? Likewise, we see God's hand in much else not at all out of the natural order. And thus in the phenomena of which we speak, it may be that God makes use of a second natural cause directed by Himself and unknown to us, or on the contrary, He may act without such intervention;

but in one of these ways, either directly by God's hand, or indirectly through a second cause acting miraculously, were they produced. Let the reader choose between the two.

Hence, what we have clearly brought to light, is a fact apparently overlooked by Father Cardellach, that the recent phenomena or new marvels of St. Teresa's heart, whether they be of natural or supernatural origin, must be attributed to a Divine Intelligence, no doubt designing by this means, to add another ray of glory to this incomparable woman's crown.

CONCLUSION.

We are approaching the termination of our little work, the aim of which has been to spread throughout Italy, and especially among St. Teresa's clients, a knowledge of the marvels (both those of our own day and those of an earlier date), the All-Powerful has wrought in the heart of Carmel's Seraph. We have acquainted our readers with aught pertaining to the question, giving a description of the most recent facts, borrowed from the authorized depositions of eyewitnesses, who were scrupulously conscientious, and took every possible precaution to ascertain the truth. We have also endeavored to penetrate the meaning of these wonders, and it is well that our interpretation of them never occurred to the mind of our excellent Spanish author, who so ingenuously specifies all the phenomena without seizing upon their signification. Had it been otherwise, some might have suspected that a strong tendency to mysticism, had helped him discóver the wool, the thorns, the branches, and other such objects. As to the solution of the problem of their miraculous nature, we have indicated the shortest, most natural and decisive way of doing so. It may be found in the answer to this question: Does there exist in nature a blind agent, chemical, vegetable, animal, of any kind whatsoever, capable of forming around the heart of St. Teresa these striking marvels, as exists the bee, author of the wonderfully symmetrical and beautiful honeycomb? Let each of our readers answer with his hand upon his heart. Had Father Cardellach put this question, he might certainly have spared himself many pages, and the objections of the Madrid priest would not have proved so very embarrassing.

We are profoundly convinced, that the wonders our contemporaries have contemplated in St. Teresa's heart, are intimately connected with important events of these later days. This heart is like a time-piece placed under a crystal bell, which gives warnings of a future, yet an enigma to us. It speaks to Spain, to the whole Catholic world, but a language that to-day no one does or can comprehend. "We speak . . . . a wisdom which is hidden." *Loquitur sapientiam in mysterio.*[1] This dust, these thorns, these threads, this wool, these grains of aromatic spices, incense and rice, these rods, are mysterious words heard by the Saint in Heaven, and which "it is not granted to man to utter." *Audivet arcana verba, quæ non licet homini loqui.*[2] They are a prophetic figure, a foreshadowing, an image of events now hidden in God, but soon, perhaps, to be revealed. The world knows well how God is wont to prepare Christian peoples for great coming events, fortunate or otherwise, by signal prodigies, and admirable phenomena, sometimes magnificent, sometimes terrible.

When Constantine the Great hastened from Gaul into Italy to combat Maxentius, the apparition of a simple cross in the heavens, was for him the signal of the first and greatest triumph of the Church, during the first twenty years of the fourth century.

May it please the Most High, through the intercession of St. Teresa, that these Wonders we have been considering, wrought by Him in

---

[1] I Cor. ii, 7.
[2] II Cor. xii, 4.

the holy Mother's heart, indeed betoken an end to this momentous situation of the Church—a situation perhaps unparalleled in her history.

Meanwhile, may our incomparable Reformatrix, from her heavenly throne, deign to accept as a tribute of devotion and love, this humble work of one of her lowliest sons, undertaken with the sole view of increasing her glory.

Note.

A letter from the Mother Prioress of the Monastery of Alba de Tormes, to Father Cardellach, written April 24, 1876, mentions new peculiarities observable in St. Teresa's heart. The first is a tube issuing from the lower part of the heart on the side of the wound, in a line descending towards the dust; it is not quite an eighth of an inch in diameter, and about one-sixth of an inch long. The second phenomenon is a notable diminution of the dust remarked by all the religious—this diminution is so great that the heart appears entirely separated from the dust, which is now seen only on the side whence issues the little tube, whose extremity disappears in the residue or sediment, supposed by many to be the origin of the great thorns. The third is, that what at first might have been taken for a silver thread, has grown much thicker, and by an artificial light, sparkles beautifully amidst the dust. The shreds of wool have become so much larger as to attract the attention of all the religious. Fourthly: Many tiny thorns discovered by Father Cardellach, with the help of a glass, are now visible to the naked eye, so that their existence can no longer be doubted, and thus every object observed by Father Cardellach is growing more distinct. The Prioress adds: "Notwithstanding the obstacle of the dust, all things seem to confirm his opinion, that the thorns spring from the lower extremity of St. Teresa's heart. Not only do we perceive more distinctly the various objects pointed out by the good Missionary, but every day this heart becomes more admirable, presenting now phenomena utterly inexplicable to myself and the other religious."

We (the compiler of this book) have written twice to Alba de Tormes, and once to the excellent Father Cardellach at Badajoz, to get the latest accounts, but we do not know whether our letters ever reached their destination, as they have not been answered.

Panegyric on St. Teresa,

DELIVERED AT FERRARA,

In the Church of St. Jerome of the Discalced Carmelite Fathers,

OCTOBER 15, 1875.

NOTE.—This panegyric appears to us calculated to add weight, to what we have advanced in regard to the thorns of St. Teresa's heart. It bears the same date as Father Cardellach's work.

Erit arcus in nubibus, et videbo illum et recordabor foederis sempiterni.

And the bow shall be in the clouds, and I shall see it, and shall remember the everlasting covenant.—GEN. ix, 16.

After the storm the bow shone resplendent in the heavens, its seven colors painted upon the clouds by the All-Powerful hand of God, as His smile, and a memento of His alliance with us. *Gyravit coelum in circuitu gloriae suae,* says Ecclesiasticus, *manus Excelsi aperuerunt illum.* "It encompasseth the Heaven about with the circle of its glory, the hands of the Most High have displayed it."[1] In the XVIth century, a wind of revolt unparalleled in history blew over Catholic Europe; the sky of the Church was surcharged with clouds, and the Master of Lies, the Prince of Apostates, unchained such a whirl-

---

[1] Eccle. xliii, 13.

wind of wrath against the Christian nations that the faithless and wicked thought the last hour of the Roman Church had surely sounded.

It was then, amidst other signs of Divine intervention, that Teresa of Jesus appeared: led by God's hand from her first Monastery of Avila, where her religious career began, to that of Alba de Tormes, where she died. Like the bow in the clouds, did she recall to the Church and her Order of Carmel, His eternal covenant with them, His promise to preserve them both, even to the end of ages. *Erit arcus in nubibus, et videbo illum, et recordabor foederis sempiterni.* Let not this eulogium appear to you excessive, nor this comparison strange, for they were employed both by the Holy Spirit in exalting the Pontiff Simon, son of Onias,[1] and the Roman Church in praise of another Spanish Saint, Elizabeth of Arragon, Queen of Portugal.

And what was the sun, my dear Brethren, whose seven colored rays, reflected upon the heart of this pure virgin, shone forth so resplendently? It was Jesus, the Light of the world, the Sun of the universe: *Et facies ejus sicut sol lucet in virtute sua.*[2] "And His face was as the sun shineth in his power." One day Jesus appeared under the form of a little child to

---
[1] Eccle. 1, 8.
[2] Apoc. i. 16.

Teresa, and asked her who she was. "I am Teresa of Jesus," was her answer, and immediately He replied: "And I, I am Jesus of Teresa." Admirable words revealing to us the light painting this rainbow of peace; the gardener working in this garden of delights; the architect who erected this living temple of the Holy Spirit; the host of this secret abode of God; the Supreme One enclosed in this tower of David, who was the honor of the Church, the glory of Spain, the marvel of the world.

And I, who am rejoiced to call her my spiritual Mother, have to-day the difficult but sweet task of inviting you to contemplate this bow in the heavens, like to that St. John saw around the throne of God—to visit this garden; to admire this fortress of sanctity elevated by the hand of the Most High. Let me give you in a few words, the tone of my discourse, the aspects under which we are to consider her. I assert that Jesus during a long work of more than sixty-five years, fashioned Teresa, by the operation of the Holy Spirit into a Spouse, a Mother, a spiritual Teacher, unique of their kind, so that the world has never seen a Teacher, a Mother, a Spouse comparable to her. Lend me your attention, and I will endeavor to convince you, that such are truly the three sovereign characteristics, under which are embraced the life, the spirit and the glory of this Saint, who is the copy of no one, and whom no one has ever been able to copy. First point: My dear Brethren, the more worthy is Teresa of eulogium, the less does she need it. Could we represent her just as she was in the eyes of God and man, panegyric were useless. Eloquent words are of slight account compared to facts. *Prolixa laudatio est,* says St. Ambrose, *quæ non quæritur, sed tenetur.*[1] Consequently, my intention is not to expatiate upon her virtues myself, but merely to place before you a faithful, accurate portrait of this holy virgin, and thus furnishing the material, let you pronounce the panegyric.

The first aspect under which we are to consider her, is that of the Spouse of Jesus, and in this she is certainly unique, not because she has surpassed all others in virtue, but because she appears the embodiment of wonders peculiar to herself. And not the least striking of these is the fact that her life, trait for trait, seems a reproduction of that of the Spouse in the Canticles, so that the book of Solomon might easily have been deemed a prophecy, admirably realized in her. Let us begin the comparison, and we will find the resemblance such as to fill us with astonishment.

Teresa was born at Avila, a beautiful city of Old Castile, March 28, 1515, under the Pontifi-

---

[1] In festo S. Agnetis, v.

cate of Leo X, and in the time of the holy and learned Father John Baptist of Mantua, just a year before Martin Luther's sacrilegious revolt. The little girl was very pretty, and her bearing so gently grave, so graciously modest, that 'ere attaining the age of reason she was called the Matron. All loved the little Teresa, though none could yet suspect that this child was destined to become in future years, as a wall of separation between Spain and the countries infested by the new heresy, against whose progress her prayers, her sighs and tears would prove a formidable obstacle; still less could they foresee, that she would be for thousands and thousands of virgins, Spanish, Portuguese, Italian, French, German, indeed of every nationality, as the blessed portal conducting them to the chamber of the Lamb. Yet the Angels had already saluted her with these words of the Sacred Canticles: " Our sister is little: if she be a wall, let us build upon it bulwarks of silver; if she be a door, let us join it together with boards of cedar." *Soror nostra parva; si est murus, ædificemus super eum propugnacula argentea; si ostium est, compingamus illud tabulis cedrinis.*[1] These ramparts of silver, what were they? For her they were the Saints, whose Lives she devoured with such eagerness in company with her little brother Rodrigo, that

---

[1] Cant. viii, 8, 9.

they both fled the paternal mansion to seek in pagan lands the crown of martyrdom, to give their lives for Jesus Christ, and thus advance the hour of their entrance into eternal glory. The tables of cedar were solitude, silence, prayer, and that great devotion to the Mother of God, remarked in the child at a tender age.

Arrested in her flight to pagan lands, she wished at least to imitate the solitaries, and aided by this same little brother, with their childish, inexperienced hands, they built in the paternal garden miniature hermitages, there to live in solitude like the hermits of old. A simple, innocent amusement, but Jesus, her future Spouse, already addressed her thus: "Hail, thou that dwellest in the gardens!" *Quae habitas in hortis.*[1] And again, whilst still a child, Teresa was wont with other children of her age, to indulge in another similar pastime, that of erecting little monasteries and playing nun, so that surrounded by her young companions, these other words from the Book of Canticles were also applicable to her: "Therefore young maidens have loved thee." *Ideo adolescentulae dilexerunt te.*[2] Losing her mother at twelve years of age, with many tears, she besought Mary to be her Mother. Though naturally inclined to piety as we have seen, too great intimacy with some of

---

[1] Cant. viii, 13.
[2] Cant. i, 2.

her worldly relatives, one young girl especially, whose spirit was that of levity and vanity, gradually infused the same sentiments into Teresa, and for a time she neglected the cultivation of the spiritual vine of her soul, she, who later would become the guardian of so many spiritual vines; she, who was to found monasteries. *Posuerunt me custodem in vineis.* " They have made me the keeper in the vineyards." Behold in these words her vocation, and in the following the fickleness of youth: *Vineam meam non custodivi:* "My vineyard I have not kept."[1] But at the age of sixteen, in the Providence of God, she was entered as a scholar (very much against her will) at a convent of Augustinian nuns, and it was here amidst these austere daughters she recovered her first fervor—*Nescivi: anima mea conturbavit me.* " I knew not: my soul troubled me."[2] Bad health prevented her remaining long in this house of education. Shortly after leaving school, she thinks of becoming the Spouse of Christ, and entering the Monastery of Carmel, at Avila. Though a step very repugnant to her nature, (how different in this respect from the majority of maidens who joyfully cross the threshold of the cloister!) Teresa, docile to grace, yields to the voice of God, and, after a terrible struggle with self, aided by her brother, she

---
[1] Cant. 1, 5.
[2] Cant. vi, 11.

escapes from her father's house and enters the Convent of the Incarnation.

This took place in 1533, the very year Henry VIII dragged Great Britain into a revolt against the Apostolic See.

And now behold Teresa wearing the Carmelite habit. The world is astonished at her flight— her father deeply afflicted and irritated.

But for ages had her response been written in the Epithalamium of Solomon : " I have put off my garment; how shall I put it on ? I have washed my feet; how shall I defile them ? " *Expoliavi me tunica mea, quomodo induar illa? lavi pedes meos, quomodo inquinabo illos?* [1] " No, no; I turn not back. Adieu, my father, my brothers, my sisters—all adieu forever!" And Teresa climbed the sacred heights of Carmel, to seat herself in the shade of that old, majestic tree of the Carmelite Order, now become her mother. But a mother, alas! already despoiled of her primitive spirit, and in these sad days cruelly wounded by schism and heresy! I read in the Annals of Carmel, that at this time, Henry VIII alone, dispersing the Carmelites in England, Scotland and Ireland, destroyed fifty-six monasteries; put to death, imprisoned and sent into exile fifteen hundred religious; and, what is worse, seduced others to heresy and corruption;

---

[1] Cant., v, 3.

so that these words of the Spouse in the Canticles were indeed applicable here: *Sub arbore malo suscitavi te: ibi corrupta est mater tua, ibi violata est genetrix tua.*[1] Nevertheless, the Order of Carmel always remained the privileged Order and family, as it were, of Mary, whom Teresa had chosen for her mother. In this second maternal abode she desired to be all for Jesus, and to become a scholar in the school of so great a Master. *Apprehendam te, et ducam in domum matris meæ: ibi me docebis.*[2] "I will take hold of thee and bring thee into my mother's house: there thou shalt teach me."

But it was written in Heaven that all the sufferings, as well as delights, all the struggles and trials mentioned in the Book of Canticles, were to be verified in Teresa in a unique manner—even as they had never been in any other. Hence, the gentle spring time of her nuptials with Jesus must be preceded by that hard, stormy winter of which the Holy Book says: "For winter is now past; the rain is over and gone. The flowers have appeared in our land." *Jam enim hiems transiit imber abiit, et recessit: flores apparuerunt in terra nostra.*[3] This terrible winter, with its hardships and severities, was for Teresa to last nearly twenty years. Long fainting spells, very

---

[1] Cant., viii, 5.
[2] Cant., viii, 2.
[3] Cant. ii, 11, 12.

acute pains in the heart, all manner of bodily sufferings, were her daily bread. Medical skill brought no relief, and one whole year, accompanied by another religious, she was obliged to be absent from the monastery and seek relief in the country. *Veni, dilecta mea, egrediemur in agrum, commoremur in villis.*[1] "Come, my beloved, let us go forth into the field; let us abide in the villages," says the Holy Book.

During this sojourn in the country, Teresa placed herself in the hands of a woman, who, though enjoying the reputation of healing all manner of infirmities, became for our poor Saint almost an executioner, by reason of her absurd remedies, especially those for the heart. Teresa was reduced to a skeleton, her disgust for every species of nourishment was extreme, and her bodily pains excruciating. It appeared to her as if sharp teeth were tearing her to pieces, the burning fever consuming her life seemed to reach the very marrow in her bones, and amidst the increasing paroxysms of torture, she could find rest neither night nor day. Her nerves were contracted most horribly, and her body bent in such a manner that she resembled a coil of ropes. Teresa even was astonished at her own patience, but knowing that it came from the Lord, she returned thanks to Him, fixing her eyes upon

---

[1] Cant. vii, 11.

holy Job, whose merits the celebrated Morals of St. Gregory had helped her to study. Whilst at her father's house, on the night of the Assumption she was taken so ill, that for four days she lay insensible, apparently dead; not only were the Last Sacraments administered, but preparations made for her burial, and she was on the point of being buried alive. She returned to her monastery, though the disease showed no signs of yielding, and for three years was a cripple, able to move about only on her hands and knees. At length recommending herself to the holy patriarch St. Joseph, his intercession obtained for her a perfect cure. The hands of this young Spouse of Jesus distilled myrrh, the exquisite myrrh of heroic patience. *Manus meae stillaverunt myrrham, et digiti mei pleni myrrha probatissima.*[1] "My hands dropped with myrrh, and my fingers were full of the choicest myrrh."

Falling into a state of spiritual languor in consequence of useless, dangerous conversations in the parlor, Jesus recalled her to Himself by a vision, in which He appeared before her bound to the pillar of flagellation; also, by the death of her beloved father. She resumed the practice of mental prayer, and for many years struggled violently against great desolation and aridity of spirit. It was truly that frightful desert through

---

[1] Cant. v, 5.

which the Spouse, by her prayers and groans, journeyed to Heaven, like "the pillar of smoke of aromatical spices of myrrh and frankincense," ascending to the skies. *Ascendit per desertum, sicut virgula fumi ex aromatibus myrrhæ et thuris.*[1] God had already made her the recipient of supernatural favors, but she bore in her soul the thorn of fear lest they were illusions, a thorn whose prickings never ceased but with life. Some individuals of more piety than judgment, did not hesitate to tell her that she was possessed by the demon, but consoled and reassured by several Fathers of the Society of Jesus, and especially St. Francis Borgia, she continued her course in the spiritual life. She meditated upon the Passion of Jesus Christ, and began to treat her body with great severity, even extending herself upon and rolling upon a bed of thorns. With an increase of Divine favors, came likewise renewed perplexities, and the doubts of her spiritual directors as to the source and nature of these favors, again caused her to be looked upon as the dupe of the demon, and she became the sport of the vulgar. In thus becoming the sport of the vulgar, she, in a measure, increased her resemblance to the Spouse of the Canticles: *et jam me nemo despiciat,*[2] "and no man may despise me." Her confessors, the guardians of

---

[1] Cant. iii, 6.
[2] Cant. viii, 1.

her soul flagellated her by their absurdities and martyrized her by their decisions. *Invenerunt me custodes, percusserunt me, et vulneraverunt me.*[1] "The keepers that go about the city found me, they struck me, and wounded me." Behold her, solitary and abandoned, sorrowfully ignorant of God's exceeding love for her. *Ignoras te, O pulcherrima inter mulieres.*[2] "Thou knowest not thyself, O fairest among women." She calls her Spouse, and there is no answer: *At ille declinaverat atque transierat.*[3] "But he had turned aside and was gone." She calls Him in the silence of the night and her cries awaken no response; she calls Him at break of day, and this day is for her as the presage of one filled with sorrow. She seeks Him in the country but finds Him not; in the church, He has fled; within the enclosure of her cell, but all in vain! Poor Teresa! *Quæsivi et non inveni illum; vocavi, et non respondit mihi.*[4] "I sought Him and found Him not: I called, and He did not answer me." Ah! brethren, the pencil falls from my fingers, unwilling to paint such woe.

But the cries of this desolate virgin penetrated the heavens.[5] Not only did John of Avila, St. Peter of Alcantara, and illustrious theologians of the Order of St. Dominic, bring consolation to her wounded soul, but the flames of Divine

---
[1] Cant. v, 7. [2] Cant. i, 7. [3] Cant. v, 6. [4] Ibid.
[5] The year 1559.

love strong and irresistible, burst forth in her heart with such impetuosity as to envelope her being, and indeed become the recompense of all she had undergone. Even the celestial spirits come to her aid; for behold she sees one day, standing at her left, an angel from Heaven, a Seraph, in his hand a golden spear with a point of fire, which he thrust at times into her heart, piercing her very entrails. The pain was exceeding great, but likewise the sweetness and celestial joy. Her heart was on fire; like a volcano, it burst forth in ardent flames mounting to Heaven, and a canticle of love gave vent to her raptures. Angels of God, suspend your melodies, listen to Teresa's hymn. And thou, lovely Seraph who hast wounded her, accompany this canticle with the murmurings of thy immortal harp. Ages ago the Holy Spirit had foretold this canticle in these words of the Spouse, which are seemingly an epitome of it: *Fulcite me floribus, stipate me malis : quia amore langueo.*[1] "Stay me up with flowers, compass me about with apples: because I languish with love."

Speaking of this favor bestowed on Teresa by an angel of light, recalls another event, the work of a spirit of darkness, as Teresa herself declares. I allude to the fall she once had from the top to the bottom of a long flight of steps. Her arm

---
[1] Cant. ii, 5.

was broken, and in consequence of a cruel, awkward setting, always remained crippled, so that she was unable to use it during the remainder of her life. Do not this wounded heart and broken arm remind you of the two seals, the Lover wishes his Spouse to wear? *Pone me ut signaculum super cor tuum, ut signaculum super brachium tuum.*[1] "Put me as a seal upon thy heart, as a seal upon thy arm." And remark, that not only are the seals placed in the order mentioned as to time, but on the same occasion, the Spouse speaks of a love strong as death, and more powerful than hell. Teresa's life was in great danger from either wound, and in the latter case, hell no doubt made an effort to end her existence. *Quia fortis est ut mors dilectio, dura sicut infernus aemulatio:*[2] "Love is strong as death, jealousy is hard as hell."

Who could henceforth doubt that Teresa was a Spouse of Jesus, unique indeed, since her life and death are so peculiarly foreshadowed in the Book of Canticles? Do you find anything like it in connection with other Saints? I have said Teresa's death as well as life were prefigured in the Book of Canticles: the Spouse eulogized by Solomon is called a dove; when Teresa died her beautiful soul was seen ascending to Heaven in the form of a dove. "Arise, make haste and

---

[1] Cant. viii, 6. [2] Ibid.

come, the flowers have appeared in the land," says the Lover in the Canticles to His Spouse: *flores apparuerunt in terra nostra.*[1] When Teresa's soul flew to its celestial Spouse, a little tree near her cell burst into bloom, though it was not then the season, neither had the tree blossomed before, nor ever did again. I repeat it, do you find such striking analogies as these in connection with any other Saint? Tell me another to whom Jesus Christ has said as He did to this favored virgin: "*If I had not created Heaven, I would have created it for thee*," or yet to whom did He ever say as to Teresa, when once she expressed her holy jealousy of Mary Magdalene, so beloved by Him: "When I was on earth, Magdalene was my cherished one, and now that I am in Heaven, I take thee for such, thou art my dear one." Hence we see that Teresa was veritably a Spouse of our Lord, unique of her kind: *Una est columba mea.*[2] She was also a child of Mary, unique of her kind: *Una est matris suae, electa genetricis suae.*[3]

Second point:—I shall now endeavor to show you, that Teresa was equally a Mother unique of her kind. But before going farther, let me describe her personal appearance. She was tall, graceful and prepossessing in her youth, characteristics of which age never robbed her. Her figure

---

[1] Cant. ii, 12.   [2] Cant. vi, 8.   [3] Ibid.

was rather full, her face round, but well-proportioned, her complexion clear and ruddy,[1] like that of the Spouse in the Canticles we have so often quoted. Her hair was black, and slightly inclined to curl, black like that of the Spouse: *Comae ejus nigrae quasi corvus.*[2] "His locks—black as a raven." Her forehead was broad and noble, her eyes black, bright and expressive, equally capable of inspiring confidence, respect and fear; veneration also was often awakened in those who looked upon her pure face, at times so radiant when in prayer, that she was even more than beautiful. Her gait was unaffected and dignified, her demeanor modest, her manners so affable and engaging as to win all hearts. It could be said of her as of the Spouse in the Canticles: "Thy lips are as a dropping honeycomb, honey and milk are under thy tongue." *Favus distillans labia tua, mel et lac sub lingua tua.*[3] Around her blessed person one was conscious of a wonderful fragrance, so that the literal application of these words to her were not inappropriate: "And the smell of thy garments is as the smell of frankincense." *Et odor vestimentorum tuorum sicut odor thuris.*[4] The qualities of her mind and heart even surpassed those of her person—she possessed a clear, penetrating, comprehensive intellect that won for her the esteem of the

---

[1] Cant. v, 10. [2] Cant. v, 11. [3] Cant. iv, 11. [4] Ibid.

learned; a courageous soul, a generous heart, sincere, grateful, gentle and considerate. She was skilful in reconciling adversaries and healing wounded friendships; knowing how to combine exquisite prudence and management with simplicity, uprightness and extraordinary candor. *Dedit ei Deus sapientiam et prudentiam multam nimis, et latitudinem cordis, quasi arenam quae est in littore maris.*[1] "And God gave to her wisdom and understanding exceeding much, and largeness of heart as the sand that is on the sea shore. Such was the holy Mother St. Teresa, the Reformatrix of degenerated Carmel.

Mother Teresa, and wherefore do we call her Mother? Because she was the Spouse of Jesus, and she would not have been a perfect Spouse, had she not also become a mother. As Mary, overshadowed by her Divine Spouse, the Holy Spirit, became the Mother of God; as the Church, Spouse of Jesus Christ, was made the Mother of all Christians: the Spouse on Calvary, the Mother at the Cenacle, even so religious, who having abandoned the world to become Spouses of Jesus Christ, thereby acquire the name of Reverend Mothers, because by their prayers, their tears and good works, they participate in the great maternity of the Church, whose chil''ren they multiply. Hence, the maternity of Teresa, the

---

[1] III Kings iv, 29.

Reformatrix of Carmel, the Mother of two religious families, was and must be the natural consequence of her nuptials with Jesus. As she was a Spouse unique of her kind, likewise was she destined to be a Mother unparalleled. One reflection alone suffices to prove this: no other woman has ever founded an Order for men, as well as one for her own sex.

And thou, bright Angel of reformed Carmel, Miracle of Christian mortification, Prodigy of mystical wisdom, John of the Cross, Honor and Light of the whole Spanish Church, thou wast surely the first and most illustrious among all Teresa's sons. As the setting sun, on a calm eve, paints upon the humid bosom of the raincharged clouds, the seven colors of the rainbow, and this in turn, is crowned by a second arch of fainter brilliancy and colors reversed, so Teresa of Jesus, herself an astonishing reflection of the glory of Christ, her Spouse, forms the spiritual life of this young hero, whose virtues were a living image of her soul, and whose voice was the echo of her own.

Let us consider the following singular circumstance, which is without parallel. The origin of the Order of Carmel is lost in the obscurity of ages, and we have every reason for believing that it dates back to that family of solitaries and prophets, of which the prophet Elias was the founder and model, as is attested by his statue in the Vatican basilica. Hence this Order is embraced in both Testaments. In the Old Testament its founder Elias appeared, shortly after a great portion of the people of Israel separated from the royal house of Juda, and refused to participate in the true worship of God in the temple of Jerusalem. In the New Testament, the Reformatrix Teresa appeared, just as a great part of Europe was torn from the Pope and the Catholic religion. Elias had in John the Baptist an heir of his spirit and powers,[1] and so had Teresa in John of the Cross. And if Elias be represented by the angel of the Apocalypse announced at the end of time,[2] no less significant of Teresa, is the rainbow encircling the angel's head.[3]

But Teresa did not become the fruitful Mother of two religious families, and consequently a mother, as we have said, unique of her kind, without tasting sufferings inexpressible. The history of what she underwent is painful in the extreme. She was ridiculed, publicly censured in the churches, even when present, and by the priests; she was reprimanded severely, and formally denounced to the Inquisition by one of the nuns of her convent, advised thereto by the confessor of the house. Elias was persecuted by the impious, but Teresa had the severer trial of being persecuted by the good, and almost entirely by the good. Her directors were against

---

[1] Luke i, 17. [2] Apoc. x, 6. [3] Apoc. x, 1.

her; she encountered the opposition of her superiors and companions in religion; she became the derision of the whole Order of the Mitigated Observance at the General Chapter of Plaisance, and the jest of nearly all Spain. *Paupercula, tempestate convulsa, absque ulla consolatione.* "O, poor little one, tossed with tempest, without all comfort."[1] We nowhere read of persecutions like these heaped upon other Foundresses. But the power of man's rage excited against Teresa, must needs yield to the impotence of this virgin, for nothing can resist God or hinder His designs. After years of excessive fatigue, trials, journeys, prayers and tears, our Saint lived to see erected thirty-two houses of her reform, seventeen for women, fifteen for men. Avila, Medina del Campo, Malagon, Valladolid, Toledo, Salamanca, Alba de Tormes, Seville, Granada, Burgos and other cities, saw arise within their walls the humble dwellings of the poor Discalced Carmelites. And though Time's destructive hand has swept away five dynasties in Spain, though revolutions have been rife in the land, and suppressions oft the order of the day, these royal houses of the Lord have ever been preserved inviolate. And now St. Teresa's two families are flourishing in nearly every quarter of the Christian world. Ah! tell me indeed if aught similar can be

---

[1] Isaias liv., 11.

said of any other Foundress, and if our holy Teresa be not incomparably worthy the appellation of Mother?

She is likewise a Teacher, unique of her kind, and here are my reasons for this assertion. The Church gives the title of wise and prudent, to all the Spouses of Jesus who have honored virginity by their heroic virtue. *Haec est virgo sapiens,* says she, *et una de numero prudentum.* But the Spouse of Eternal Wisdom, unique of her kind, must be so exceeding wise and prudent as to have no equals, and such Teresa truly was. As the orb of night clothed with the reflections of the sun, for the first few days timidly displays its silver bow in the sky, but gradually increasing in size and brilliancy, at length from the heights of heaven's vaults shines resplendent over the face of the earth: so Teresa of Jesus, eagerly turning towards the Source of light; "passing," as St. Paul says, "from brightness to brightness;" borne by the Holy Spirit, by degrees became an astonishing reflection of Divine wisdom, and a Teacher for the faithful, receiving her instructions direct from God.

In three different ways did Teresa become truly a spiritual Teacher. First: By the superior influence of her virtues and the light of her heroic example, she became a Teacher of the spiritual life to all Christians, but especially religious. Indeed, what faith must have been hers, who could truthfully say she would rather suffer death a thousand times, than to see the least ceremony of the Church violated! How great the hope of this grand soul, how great her confidence and abandonment into the hands of God, even when He seemed unmindful of her, turning a deaf ear to the urgent necessities of His Spouse, and coming to her assistance only in the last extremity, after she had fully reached the bitterness of long and anxious waiting! How excessive the love for her sole and Supreme Good, which could transform her heart into an ardent volcano; that heart so avaricious of suffering, and whose heroic cry was to suffer or to die: *"aut pati, aut mori!"* What charity and compassion for the erring! Often her soul was overcome by grief, and she dissolved in tears, at thoughts of so many of God's creatures still wrapped in the shades of infidelity and heresy. She had a jealous care of her neighbor's reputation, and a warm place in her heart for the poor and infirm. But what can we say of her love for the Blessed Sacrament? The favors she received at the foot of the altar were extraordinary; frequently her Communions were followed by ecstacies; and after death, though realizing the bliss of Heaven, she appeared to one of her spiritual daughters and recommended especially great devotion to our Lord in the Eucharist. And what of her love for the Blessed

Virgin, who so often appeared to her, and of her devotion to the angels and saints of both Testaments? How describe her filial affection for and unshaken confidence in the Patriarch St. Joseph, whose apostle she became throughout the Catholic world? For is it not owing to Teresa and her celebrated promises, that the universal Protector of the Church is he, who was her own especial assistant and friend—that the tutelary angel of her two families, should become that of all Christian peoples, and that the patron of the poor virgin of Avila, should be constituted the patron of the grand poor man of the Vatican? And again, what exceeding prudence, what scrupulous justice, what strength, what an exquisite odor of spotless temperance and angelic chastity beamed from this soul, which was never sullied with a grave fault! Who can measure the exactitude of her obedience; her affection for angelic poverty; her recollection in prayer; her invincible patience amidst every species of trial; and above all, who can sound the depths of her humility, that solid foundation of this imposing spiritual edifice?

She merited likewise to teach the world, by reason of her experience of those gifts of God bestowed upon certain privileged souls—gifts which in her case were unexampled, continuous, innumerable. What a sea of wonders this subject presents to our view! For what mortal indeed could describe these different sublime states of prayer, in which, elevated to a participation in Divine things, she filled Heaven and earth with those "cries and groans unspeakable," of which the Apostle writes? What could we say of those visions sometimes imaginary, more frequently intellectual, in which Mary, the angels and saints gave her glimpses of their glorified beauty? How recount those frequent ecstacies, those mysterious flights of the soul, those raptures, those magnanimous outbursts of love for God, as if this pure mortal longed only to be united to the Divinity and wholly absorbed therein? Which of us can have the faintest idea of those sublime visions of the Trinity, with which she was favored; that clear comprehension at times of secrets hidden in the bosom of the future; of those sweet, refreshing and miraculous conversations, that from a desert of troubles immediately transported her to a garden of delights? Behold, now, from all we have said, why she has merited, by her experience of all these wonders, to become the Teacher of Teachers, even of mystical theology, in a degree far surpassing that of other virgins who had been the recipient of supernatural favors. To his shame be it said of the bold, blasphemous author of the famous "Life of Jesus," that in speaking of Teresa, he has dared treat her revelations as phantasies of the imagination. Ah! the enemy of Jesus could never be a friend to His virgin Spouse!

And finally, she taught the world by her admirable writings, composed without study or preparation, not even re-read or revised, and written often with a radiant face and a halo around her head. These works are evident proof, that her knowledge was the infused gift of the Holy Spirit, according to the prophecy of Joel and Christ's promises to His Apostles. In the "History of Her Life," written in obedience to her confessors; in the "Way of Perfection;" in the famous "Interior Castle;" in her "Book of Foundations;" in the "Constitutions" of her religious; in the collections of her "Letters;" in her shorter compositions, such as those upon the "Canticle of Canticles," the "Pater Noster" and other subjects, we perceive such a degree of ascetic doctrine and mystical science, as has certainly never been attained by any other woman. And in reading her posthumous work conceived in Paradise, that is, the "Counsels" she gave from Heaven when enlightened by the Divine Essence, we notice the great resemblance between the writings of Teresa, a pilgrim on earth, and Teresa, the blessed in Heaven, which strikes us especially as incontestable and beautiful proof, that God who enlightens her now in the plentitude of her glory, was likewise the Source whence she reflected the wisdom of her earthly material aurora. Now tell me, my hearers, if among all the illustrious virgins in the annals of the Church, you find one combining in so high a degree these three qualifications of a Teacher. As for myself, I can certainly answer that I have not.

Such, O my brethren, was Teresa of Jesus, whom I have attempted to place before you not in panegyric, but as she really was, though I am conscious of having traced her portrait in feeble colors. Full of merits more than days, she died amidst her religious at Alba de Tormes, (where her mortal remains now repose) aged sixty-seven years, six months and one week, on the 4th of October, 1582, a day memorable as marking the reform of the Gregorian calendar. Wonderful signs had preceded her death: just a little before it happened, Anne of St. Bartholomew, her friend and favorite daughter in religion, saw our Redeemer surrounded by the angels and saints, descend from Heaven to take her thence. Her happy death was likewise followed by many apparitions; she was seen in Heaven, sometimes among the Seraphim, sometimes among the Doctors of the Church. Having now exhausted my triple subject, I would here end my discourse, did I not wish to enframe the portrait presented to you; for this purpose, let us make in spirit a pilgrimage to the tomb of this most holy woman.

We are now at Alba de Tormes in the Diocese

of Salamanca. This little spot in the kingdom of Leon, is like Assisium in Umbria. If the latter city be sacred because it possesses the ashes of St. Francis, upon whose members a Seraph imprinted the Sacred Stigmata, none the less so is Alba de Tormes, where rests the body of St. Teresa whose heart was wounded by a Seraph. These two Seraphic Saints, strongly resembling and yet strongly differing, though at a great distance from one another, ascended to Heaven the same day.

What grand thoughts are awakened within us at the venerated tomb of the Virgin of Castile! Where now are the ashes of the Roman cohorts, that Scipio and Cæsar led to victory in these lands? Where rest the mortal remains of the heroes of those great wars? Who goes to place an *ex-voto* at the almost forgotten tombs of the grand Consalvo, Ferdinand Cortez or the terrible Duke of Alba? Yet the honors Catholic pilgrims render to the body of St. Teresa are incomparable, for she is the grandest woman Spain ever produced.

Her body still flexible, incorrupt, and in a state of perfect preservation, is enclosed in a double ornamented urn of crystal, and under the charge of her nuns. But the Spanish pilgrim loves especially to visit the favored reliquary enshrining her blessed heart, surrounded by thorns, and still displaying the wound of the Seraph. Let us compare Teresa's heart with that of Jesus, as the latter appeared to the blessed Margaret Mary, on the Feast of St. John the Baptist: both are wounded, both burned by fire, both bearing the sign of the cross, both surrounded by thorns. Are not the points of resemblance very strong, my brethren, and such as we have never seen in the heart of any other Saint?

Might we venture to say that as no other woman's heart ever loved Jesus so ardently, neither did any so strongly resemble His own? I would not like to affirm this, nor could I deny it.

Before this blessed urn, over which the rapacious hand of the Revolution has passed, despoiling it of its richest gifts, let us make another reflection. The grandest desires of a woman's heart are three in number; the first and strongest is to become a spouse; when a spouse, she longs to be a mother; once a mother, her ambition seeks its gratification in becoming the teacher of her children, and oftimes of those of others. And she whose life embraces this threefold duty, can seek no farther, she is all that she can be. Hence, Jesus loving Teresa would satisfy in a high degree these three inclinations of her woman's heart; wherefore, He made her a Spouse, a Mother and a Teacher unique in her kind. Casting a glance upon the history of virgins, the most holy and famous, we find none combining these three states. St. Clare of Assisium was the Spouse of Christ and the Mother of numberless virgins, but she was not a Teacher, she left no writings for the instruction of others. St. Catherine of Sienna was a Spouse and Teacher, but neither Foundress nor Mother. Nor did Gertrude, Magdalene of Pazzi, or Catherine of Bologna wear this triple crown. To whom or what then may we compare our holy Reformatrix?

In Rome, Eternal city, beyond the Tiber, and facing a magnificent square, arises the basilica of St. Peter's, one of the wonders of the world. Three cupolas majestically rear their heads, but that in the centre seems to receive the homage of the other two. In front of this great mass, whose four rows of columns remind us of two arms stretched out to encircle the place, arises massive and erect, the colossal obelisk of Sixtus V, surmounted by the cross, apparently looking in astonishment upon this marvelous work of art.

Pardon the comparison, my hearers, but if it be true that the Christian, the just, and with greater reason the saints are, according to the Apostle's words, the temple of God, may I not compare Teresa to this imposing mass of the Vatican, in which, March 12, 1625, Gregory XV decreed her the honors of a solemn canonization?

These three cupolas represent to me this grand woman in her threefold aspect of Spouse of Jesus, Mother of the new solitaries of Carmel, and Teacher of the spiritual life; the two extended arms of the great temple typifying her boundless charity embracing the whole world; and this obelisk of marble from Heliopolis, surmounted by a cross, bringing to mind the image of Teresa's great son, John of Ypes, who took the name of John of the Cross; a man as unshaken and undaunted by the winds of persecution and contradiction, as is this Egyptian monolith unmoved by the storms that pass over and around it.

But it is time we leave the tomb and its venerated relics; as a memento of our visit and a token of homage to so great a heroine, I write the following:

St. Ignatius of Loyola, a contemporary and compatriot of St. Teresa, canonized the same day as herself, declares that when in solitude at Manresa, just after his conversion, the plenitude of Divine grace flooding his heart was sufficient of itself to have made him lay down his life for the Faith, even had it lacked the testimony of the Scriptures. *Si sacrae litterae non extarent, se tamen pro fide mori paratum, ex iis solum, quae sibi Manresae patefecerat Dominus.* In like manner do I declare, that to believe in the religion of Jesus Christ, it suffices me that this religion should have given to the world Teresa of Jesus.

SHORT NOTICES
Upon the Centenary of St. Teresa.

I. There is formed in Italy, a Committee charged with promoting the feasts of the Centenary in honor of St. Teresa, to be celebrated in October, 1882, just three hundred years after her blessed death. The principal seat of this Committee is at Ferrara, in the Monastery of the Discalced Carmelite Fathers, near the Church of St. Jerome, which they serve.

II. The following are the names of the Promoters:

His Excellency, the Most Reverend Mgr. Frederico Mascaretti, of the Order of Discalced Carmelites, former Bishop of Susa.

Don Giovanni Bonnetti, Priest of the Congregation of St. Francis de Sales, at Turin.

Don Leopoldo Bulfolini, editor of *L'Etoile du Carmel*, at Sienna.

The Rev. Father Andrea of St. Joseph, a Carmelite, at Ferrara.

The Bartola Brothers, typographers at Plaisance.

Don Giacomo Murena, of the Congregation of the Mission, Ferrara.

The Rev. Father Venant of the Cross, Carmelite, Venice.

The Rev. Father Filippo of St. Bernard, Carmelite, at Trezzo d'Odda (Milan).

The Rev. Father Rafael Ballerini, of the Society of Jesus, Florence.

The Rev. Father Rafael, Carmelite, at Arezzo.

III. By this celebration it is intended not only to honor St. Teresa individually, but likewise her vocation of Spouse of Christ, and to convoke in spirit, at least throughout Italy, all cloistered virgins to an observance of the solemnities in commemoration of the three hundredth anniversary of her death. All religious will be invited, no matter to what Order they belong, to prepare for this great festival by novenas, triduos, and other especial devotions, so that it may be said of St. Teresa in these blessed days, "Her daughters saw her and declared her most blessed," (Cant. vi, 8) thus completing the resemblance between Teresa and the Spouse of the Canticles.

IV. It has also been deemed advisable, to call upon the journals best calculated for that purpose, to aid in preparing all Italy for the most solemn celebration of this Centenary. The two apparently most suitable, are the *Unita Cattolica* of Turin, which has a wide circulation, and has always lent a helping hand to other Centenaries, and *L'Etoile du Carmel*, so intimately connected with the cause of the holy Reformatrix. This will be the official organ of the festival; it appears weekly at Sienna; is a sheet of sixteen pages, etc., etc.

Let us make every effort that the triumph of this great Saint in 1882 be worthy of her, of Catholic piety, of Christian Italy, which has opened so many houses for her sons and daughters, and let us pray that on this solemn occasion all the faithful rival one another in zeal and fervor.

THE END.

www.ingramcontent.com/pod-product-compliance
Lightning Source LLC
Chambersburg PA
CBHW020923230426
43666CB00008B/1550